CHARISMA

VS.

CHARISMANIA
Chuck Smith

HARVEST HOUSE PUBLISHERS
Eugene, Oregon 97402

CHARISMA VS. CHARISMANIA

Copyright © 1983 by Harvest House Publishers
Eugene, Oregon 97402

Library of Congress Catalog Card Number 82-082241
ISBN 0-89081-353-1

Printed in the United States of America.

To all those dear saints of God who loved me and encouraged me as their pastor during the first seventeen years of my ministry, as I was struggling to do the works of God with the abilities of my flesh—those previous people who were so patient with me in my own transition from *charismania* to *charisma*.

CONTENTS

1

Searching for the Answer

I spent much of my childhood and adolescent years trying to prove I was normal even though I didn't go to movies or dances. In the Pentecostal church I attended, movies and dancing were considered horrible sins.

Since I couldn't join my friends in their worldly activities, I asked them to attend church with me, for we were constantly being exhorted to witness for Christ by bringing friends to church. The problem was that almost every Sunday the pastor would warn of the evils of Hollywood, dancing, drinking, and smoking. He used to say, "If God wanted man to smoke, He would have put a chimney on top of his head." Besides this, the service was always interrupted by two or three "messages in tongues" and interpretations.

Many times as I was seated with my unsaved friends that I had brought to church, Mrs. Newman would start her funny breathing. I had learned that this was the prelude to her speaking in tongues, so I would quickly pray, "Oh, God, please don't speak in tongues today; my friends won't understand." Either God wasn't hearing me or Mrs. Newman wasn't listening to God, because she would stand up, shaking all over, and deliver God's message for the day in a loud, high-pitched voice. I would die inside as my friends giggled beside me. I hoped they weren't committing the unpardonable sin.

I was always tense after the service as I waited for my friends to ask the inevitable question, "What was that?" I had a hard time explaining it because I didn't fully understand it myself.

As a child I couldn't help but wonder about these "messages in tongues" that I heard. Sometimes a short message was followed by a long interpretation or else a long message was followed by a short interpretation. At other times I would notice repeated phrases in the message in tongues and wonder why there weren't correspondingly repeated phrases in the interpretations.

The Mounting Questions

There were other things that bothered me about the church I attended. I wondered why, if we were the most spiritual church in town and had the most power, the other churches had so many more members. I was told that most people were looking for an easy way to heaven, and that the other churches were larger because they told the people what they wanted to hear. If our church did that, it would be full too—of people bound for hell.

Another problem I had with our church was its lack of love. I knew that the fruit of the Spirit is love, so I couldn't understand why there were so many church splits. It seemed that there were always some members who wanted to get rid of the pastor and others who supported him. People left our church so often that, if all the former members of the church returned, we would have had the largest church in town!

Somehow, leaving our church was tantamount to leaving the Lord. Those who had left had surely backslidden in their search for an easier way to heaven. However, I often found myself wishing I could go to the Community Church or the Presby-terian Church. Then on Sunday night I would feel convicted for my desire to "backslide," and I would go forward to the altar and get "saved" again.

I tried to prove that I was normal by excelling in school. I worked to be the smartest kid in the class, the fastest runner in the school, and the one who could hit the ball farther than anyone else. Unfor-tunately, most of the other kids in my Sunday school class tried to prove they were normal by smoking, drinking, and running around with the tough gangs at school. Very few of them remained in Sunday school past junior high. Through the grace of God, and with deeply committed parents, I somehow survived.

The Results of My Quest

As strange as it may seem, I am convinced today that the dead orthodoxy of many churches could be enhanced by the gifts of the Holy Spirit in opera-tion within the body—not the unscriptural excesses I observed as a child, but in a solid, Scriptural way, with the Word of God as the final authority guiding our faith and practice.

With this in mind, I began a search of the Scrip-tures for a sound, balanced approach to the Holy Spirit and His work in the church today. There must be a middle position between the Pentecostals, with their overemphasis on experience, and the fun-damentalists, who, in their quest to be right, in too many cases have become *dead* right. The results of my quest are recorded in part in this book, which I pray that God might use to lead you into the fullness of the Spirit-filled life.

Charisma is a beautiful, natural anointing of God's Spirit upon a person's life, enabling him or her to do the work of God. It is that special dynamic of

God's Spirit by which a person seems to radiate God's glory and love.

Charismania is an endeavor in the flesh to simulate charisma. It is any effort to do the work of the Spirit in the energies or abilities of the flesh—the old, selfish nature of a person. It is a spiritual hype that substitutes perspiration for inspiration. It is the use of the genius, energy and gimmicks of man as a substitute for the wisdom and ability of God. It can be demonstrated in such widely divergent forms as planning and strategy sessions, devising programs for church growth, raising funds for the church budget, or wild and disorderly outbursts in tongues that disrupt the Sunday-morning message. Whatever lacks a sound Biblical basis and demonstrates a lack of trust in the Holy Spirit to accomplish His purposes in the church apart from the devices and abilities of man is the work of the flesh.

The Balanced Position

This book will seek to present a Scripturally balanced position between the detractors who say "The devil makes them do it" and the fanatics who say "The Holy Spirit made me do it." It will also show who the Holy Spirit is and will describe His proper work in the world, the church, and the life of the believer.

We do not ask you to blindly accept all the premises, but we encourage you to search the Scriptures to see if these things are so. "Prove all things and hold fast that which is good."

2

The Holy Spirit Is God

Since the purpose of this book is to bring you into a full, personal, and soundly Biblical relationship with God the Holy Spirit, we need to first show that the Holy Spirit is one of the three Persons of the Godhead.

The church has accepted throughout its history that there is one God who exists in three Persons: the Father, the Son, and the Holy Spirit. In the Scriptures we find Them working together in total harmony for the redemption of man. Paul confessed to Timothy that the Godhead was a great mystery; for us to try to *fully* comprehend it is a futile expenditure of mental energy.

Many cult groups (such as Jehovah's Witnesses) take advantage of this gulf between the finite and the infinite to attack the triunity of God by denying the deity of Jesus Christ and passing off the Holy Spirit as an essence. Other groups deny the existence of the Father and the Holy Spirit, and say that Jesus alone is God. One of the common marks of every cult is a denial of the deity of Jesus Christ and the Person of the Holy Spirit.

The Triune God

Because this is one of the areas that the enemy constantly attacks, we must affirm not only the fact of the deity of the Holy Spirit, but also why we believe in His deity. The word "trinity" is not found in the Bible, but it is a convenient term that theologians use to describe the three Persons of the one God. Perhaps the term *triunity* would more accurately describe God. He is not $1 + 1 + 1 = 3$, but $1 \times 1 \times 1 = 1$.

In Genesis 1:1 we read, "In the beginning God...." The Hebrew word translated "God" is *Elohim*, which is plural for *El* (God in the singular). In Hebrew there is a singular, dual, and plural tense. "God" in the singular is *El*, in the dual is *Elah*, and in the plural is *Elohim*. There can be no denying that the word "Elohim" at least suggests the triunity of God.

Continuing in Genesis 1:2 we read, "the Spirit of God moved upon the face of the waters." The Holy Spirit is the first Person of the Godhead to be identified separately in the Bible. In Genesis 1:26 we read, "And Elohim said, Let *us* make man in *our* image, after *our* likeness." He did not say, "*I* will make man after *my* image." In other words, the three Persons of the Godhead were speaking jointly.

The Attributes of the Spirit

To establish that the Holy Spirit is God, we will first show that attributes which can be ascribed to God alone are ascribed to the Holy Spirit. One of the divine attributes is the eternal nature of God. He has always existed. In Hebrews 9:14 we read that Christ through the *eternal* Spirit offered Himself without spot to God. If the Spirit is eternal, and this is an attribute that can only be ascribed to deity, then the

Spirit is God. Notice also how the three Persons of the Trinity are linked in the verse.

Another attribute of God is His omniscience. God knows all things, as James said in Acts 15:18: "Known unto God are all His works from the beginning of the world." This attribute is also ascribed to the Holy Spirit. In 1 Corinthians 2:10,11 we read, "But God hath revealed them unto us by His Spirit. For the Spirit searcheth all things, yea, the deep things of God. For what man knoweth the things of a man save the spirit of man which is in him? Even so the things of God knoweth no man, but the Spirit of God." Here the knowledge of God is attributed to the Spirit of God.

Another attribute of deity is omnipresence. God exists everywhere in the universe at once. In Psalm 139:7 David asks, "Whither shall I go from Thy Spirit? Or whither shall I flee from Thy presence?" God exists in the heavens, in hell, and in the uttermost parts of the sea. The Spirit is with me now where I am, and at the same time He is with you wherever you may be reading this book right now.

God is omnipotent. This is a word used to express that He is all-powerful. When Sarah laughed at the announcement that she was to have a son in her old age, the angel of the Lord asked, "Is anything too hard for the Lord?" (Genesis 18:14). Jesus said, "With God all things are possible" (Mark 10:27). In Luke 1:37 He said, "With God nothing shall be impossible." The angel said to Mary when she questioned him on how she, a virgin, could bear a child, "The Holy Spirit shall come upon thee and the *power of the Highest* shall overshadow thee" (Luke 1:35). Here the Holy Spirit and the power of the highest are used synonymously.

The Works of the Spirit

Not only are divine *attributes* ascribed to the

Holy Spirit, but so are divine *works*. One of the divine works is that of creation. The entire Trinity was active in creation. In Genesis 1:1 we read, "In the beginning Elohim created the heavens and the earth." In John 1:1-3 we read, "In the beginning was the Word, and the Word was with God, and the Word was God. All things were made by Him, and without Him was not anything made that was made." The Spirit was also an active force in creation. In Genesis 1:2 the Spirit is described as moving over the face of the waters. The Spirit was in conference with the Father and the Son when God said, "Let us make man in *our* likeness" (Genesis 1:26). In Psalm 104:30 we read, "Thou sendest forth Thy Spirit, they are created."

Another work of God is that of giving life. We recognize that God is the Giver and Sustainer of life. In 2 Corinthians 3:6, as Paul was referring to the letter of the law, he said, "The letter killeth, but the Spirit giveth life." In John 6:63 Jesus said, "It is the Spirit that maketh alive."

The Bible was written by the inspiration of the Holy Spirit, yet we properly refer to the Bible as the Word of God. Second Peter 1:21 tells us, "For the prophecy came not in old time by the will of man, but holy men of God spoke as they were moved by the Holy Spirit." In 2 Timothy 3:16 Paul declares, "All Scripture is given by inspiration of God." Peter says that the writers were moved by the Holy Spirit and Paul says that they were inspired by God. Thus the Spirit is recognized to be God.

This is why many Scriptures in the Old Testament which declare that *the Lord* spoke are attributed to the Holy Spirit when quoted in the New Testament. In Isaiah 6:8,9 the prophet said, "I heard the voice of the Lord, saying, Whom shall I send, and who will go for *us*? Then said I, 'Here am I; send me.'

And He said, Go, and tell this people, ye hear indeed but understand not; ye see indeed but perceive not." When Paul quoted this passage in Acts 28:25,26 he said, "Well spoke the Holy Spirit by Isaiah the prophet unto our fathers, saying, '...hearing ye shall hear and not understand; seeing ye shall see and not perceive.' " Isaiah said the Lord spoke; Paul said the Holy Spirit spoke. They can both be right only if the Holy Spirit and the Lord are one.

The Trinity Working Together

In Acts 5:1-11 we have an interesting account of discipline in the infant church as God was seeking to preserve its purity. Motivated by love, many Christians attempted to establish a Christian community by selling all their possessions and turning the proceeds over to the apostles, so that the Christians might have all things in common. A certain couple, Ananias and Sapphira, sold their property but together decided to hold back a share of the price for themselves. When Ananias brought his portion to Peter, Peter asked, "Why has Satan filled your heart to lie to the Holy Spirit, and to keep part of the price of the land? While it remained was it not your own? And after it was sold, was it not in your own power? Why have you conceived this thing in your heart? You have not lied to men, but to God" (Acts 5:3,4). Peter said that Satan had filled Ananias's heart to lie to the Holy Spirit, then declared that he had lied to *God*, thereby making the Holy Spirit and God one.

Throughout the New Testament we see the Trinity working together or coupled together. When Jesus commissioned the disciples to go out and teach all nations (Matthew 28:19,20), He told them to baptize into the name of the Father, and of the Son, and of the Holy Spirit. These three names distinguish the three Persons of the one God.

In 2 Corinthians 13:14, in his apostolic benediction, Paul said, "The grace of the Lord Jesus Christ, and the love of God, and the communion of the Holy Spirit be with you all. Amen." Here again the three Persons of the one God are linked together.

In 1 Corinthians 12:4-6 Paul says, "Now there are diversities of gifts, but the same *Spirit*. And there are differences of administrations, but the same *Lord*. And there are diversities of operations, but it is the same *God* who works all in all." In verse 4 he refers to the Spirit, in verse 5 to the Lord (Jesus), and in verse 6 to God (the Father). So, though there may be diversities in the gifts and in their operation and administration, there is a unity because God is behind it all.

Access Through the Spirit

At this point you may be thinking, "Well, what difference does it all make whether the Spirit is God or just an essence from God?" Because the Spirit is a part of the Godhead, it is proper to worship Him, and we are correct when we sing, "Praise Father, Son, and Holy Ghost." God has ordained that we relate to Him through the Spirit. It is in the realm of the Spirit that man can touch God. It is my spirit brought into union with the Holy Spirit. Jesus said, "God is a Spirit, and they that worship Him *must* worship Him in Spirit and in truth" (John 4:24). Paul also said, "His Spirit bears witness with our spirits" (Romans 8:16). If I am to have communion with God, I must recognize the Holy Spirit and realize that He is the One that makes this fellowship possible.

Man has never had direct access to the Father; this is a common fallacy among people who forget the awesome holiness of God. When God manifested

Himself on the Holy Mount to the Jewish people (Exodus 19), He had them set boundaries around the mountain so they wouldn't get too close to the manifestation of God and be put to death. When the people saw from afar the awesome demonstration of God, they said to Moses, "You speak to us and we will hear, but don't let God speak to us lest we die."

The veil in the tabernacle demonstrated the separation that must exist between the Holy God and an unholy people. This veil could only be penetrated after an elaborate cleansing and sacrifices by the high priest, and this only one day in the year, and by the one man, the high priest.

Jesus said, "No man comes to the Father but by me" (John 14:6). Jesus told the Jews that they really didn't know the Father. He also told them that Moses would be the witness against them. They do not follow the prescribed way to God that was given to Moses by God, but today seek to approach Him on the basis of their good works without sacrifice.

Sin has always been the barrier between man and God, and until something is done about man's sin, there can be no approach to God. In Isaiah 59:1,2 we read, "Behold, the Lord's hand is not shortened that it cannot save; neither His ear heavy that it cannot hear; but your inequities have separated between you and your God, and your sins have hid His face from you, that He will not hear." Jesus provided a way to cleanse us from our sins, thus making the approach to God possible. Through faith in Jesus Christ my spirit is made alive, and thus can be united with God's Spirit. In this way God and man are joined in the Spirit.

3

The Person of the Holy Spirit

Because we want you to have a personal encounter with the Holy Spirit, we will next show that the Scriptures teach that the Holy Spirit is a Person, rather than merely an essence, force, or power. You can have raw power without personality, such as electricity, but it is difficult to have an intimate, close relationship to such impersonal power.

The word "spirit" in Greek is *pneuma*, which is in the neuter gender. Because of this, in early church history a brilliant theologian named Arius began to promote the idea that Jesus was less than God, having been created by God, and that the Holy Spirit is just the "essence" of God. This became known as the Arian heresy, and it still exists and attracts a wide following. The Nicaean Counsel stripped Arius from his position and branded his teachings as heresy. The Holy Spirit is more than just an essence or force; He is a Person. You shouldn't worship a force or essence. Can you imagine singing the doxology, "Praise Father, Son, and Essence"? He is a Person, and as one of the Persons of the Godhead He is worthy to be praised. If we do not believe in the personality of the Holy Spirit, we deny Him the praise and worship due Him. If we do not realize that the Holy Spirit is a Person, we find ourselves in the position of seeking to relate to a force or essence. We would be saying, "I need to yield my life to it," or, "I need more of it in my life."

Knowing, Acting, Feeling

That He is a Person is clearly shown in the Scriptures. Characteristics are ascribed to Him that can only be ascribed to persons. A person is a being with a mind, will, and feelings. If in the Scriptures these characteristics are ascribed to the Holy Spirit, then it must be concluded that the Spirit is a Person. In 1 Corinthians 2:10,11 we read, "But God hath revealed them unto us by His Spirit, for the Spirit searcheth all things, yea, the deep things of God. For what man knoweth the things of a man save the spirit of man which is in him? Even so the things of God knoweth no man, but the Spirit of God." Here reference is made to the Spirit possessing knowledge. Raw force or power possesses no knowledge. It would be absurd to replace the word "essence" for "Spirit" in the text, for you would have the "essence" searching all things!

In Romans 8:27 Paul says, "And He that searcheth the hearts knoweth what is the mind of the Spirit because He maketh intercession for the saints according to the will of God." Here reference is made to the *mind* of the Spirit, a characteristic not associated with just an essence. In 1 Corinthians 12:11 Paul, concerning the gifts of the Spirit, says, "But all these worketh that one and selfsame Spirit, dividing to each man severally as He wills." So the Holy Spirit possesses a *will*, a trait associated with personality.

In Romans 15:30 Paul associates the emotion of love to the Spirit. A force or power cannot love. You do not associate love apart from personality. It is interesting that, although I have read or heard scores of sermons on God's love, or the love of Jesus Christ for us, I have yet to hear a sermon on the love of the Holy Spirit. Yet this must be one of the chief characteristics of the Spirit, as this is the fruit He produces in our lives. The Holy Spirit does possess feelings and can be grieved, because Paul in Ephesians 4:30 admonishes the church not to grieve the Holy Spirit of God. Think how foolish it would sound to say you have grieved the essence!

The Personal Words

Throughout the Scriptures personal pronouns are used to refer to the Holy Spirit. In John 14:16 Jesus said, "And I will pray the Father, and He shall give you another Comforter, that He may abide with you forever." Here the pronoun "He" is used for both the Father and the Spirit. If you believe in a personal God, you should also believe in a personal Spirit. In that same passage Jesus went on to say that the world could not receive the Spirit because they did not see *Him* or know *Him;* Jesus said that you know *Him,* for *He* dwells with you.

Notice how many times Jesus uses the personal pronoun for the Holy Spirit. In John 16:7-14 Jesus repeatedly uses the personal pronoun to refer to the Holy Spirit. "Nevertheless, I tell you the truth: It is expedient for you that I go away, for if I go not away, the Comforter will not come unto you; but if I depart I will send *Him* unto you. And when *He* is come, *He* will reprove the world of sin, and of righteousness, and of judgment: of sin, because they believe not on me; of righteousness, because I go to my Father, and ye see me no more; of judgment, because the prince of this world is judged. I have yet many things to say unto you, but ye cannot bear them now. Howbeit when *He,* the Spirit of truth, is come, *He* will guide you into all truth: for *He* shall not speak of *Himself*; but whatsoever *He* shall hear, that shall *He* speak: and *He* will show you things to come. *He* shall glorify me: for *He* shall receive of mine, and shall show it unto you. All things that the Father hath are mine: therefore said I, that *He* shall take of mine, and shall show it unto you." In the Greek, the personal pronouns "He" and "Him" are used for the Spirit over and over in Scripture.

The Spirit in Action

Personal acts are ascribed to the Holy Spirit in the Scriptures. In Acts 13:2 we read, "The Holy Spirit said, Separate me Barnabas and Saul for the work whereunto I have called them." Again, to insert "power" or "essence" for the Spirit is incomprehensible. How can an essence or power speak? In Romans 8:26 we are told that the Holy Spirit Himself makes intercession for us with groanings which cannot be uttered. Again, try to conceive a mere force making intercession! If the Holy Spirit were just an essence or force where He is mentioned in Scripture, you should be able to insert the words "force" or "essence" and do no damage to the meaning of the text. But such a thing is obviously impossible, because the Holy Spirit is a Person. The Holy Spirit testifies of Jesus Christ in John 15:26, and He teaches the believers and brings things to their remembrance in John 14:26. In Acts 16:2,7 the Holy Spirit forbade Paul and his companions to go into Asia and would not allow them to go into Bithynia. In Genesis 6:3 we find that the Holy Spirit strives with man.

The Holy Spirit can receive treatment as a *Person*. He can be offended. It is impossible to conceive of offending "the power" or "the breath." Your breath can be offensive, but you can't offend your breath! In Ephesians 4:30 Paul exhorts, "Grieve not the

Holy Spirit of God." The Holy Spirit can be lied to. This is the accusation that Peter brought against Ananias: "You have lied to the Holy Spirit." It is also possible to blaspheme the Holy Spirit. Jesus said that this was such a heinous sin that there was no forgiveness for the person who did it. He said, "You can blaspheme me and be forgiven, but not the Holy Spirit." Here Jesus makes the distinct separation between Himself and the Holy Spirit.

The Holy Spirit is identified with persons. Paul said, "It seemed good to the Holy Spirit and to us" (Acts 15:28). Try making sense by inserting wind or power in this verse!

The Holy Spirit is a Person; He is not just the essence of God. You need to come into a personal relationship with Him so that you might begin to experience His love and His power working in your life as He guides you in your spiritual walk.

The Power of the Spirit

Have you ever felt that you should share with a person his or her need to accept Jesus Christ, yet you didn't have the nerve to bring up the subject? Have you ever gone past a college, observed the thousands of students, realized that most of them are lost, and then wondered how they could possibly be reached for Christ? Do you ever think of the billions of people who have never received a true presentation of the gospel, and then wonder how it might be accomplished?

To Peter, who denied his Lord on a one-to-one basis with the young maid, and to the rest of the disciples (who fled when the going got tough) the commission of Jesus to go into all the world and preach the gospel to every creature must have seemed a totally impractical as well as an impossible command, and indeed it was. There is no way that 11 insignificant men from Galilee could reach the world for Jesus Christ. That is why Jesus told them to wait in Jerusalem until they received the *power of the Holy Spirit,* for it was by this power that they were to be witnesses to the uttermost parts of the world.

Is this experience of the power of the Holy Spirit something that God intended only for the early church? Do the Scriptures indicate that the time would come when we did not need to depend on the power of the Spirit, but through our perfected knowledge of the Scriptures we could do God's work on our own? Is the church that was begun in the Spirit now to be perfected in the flesh? What is the answer to the church's impotence? Why has the church failed to stop the mad downward plunge of the corrupted world around us?

Paul warns us in Hebrews 4 to fear that we do not come short of receiving the promise of God to enter into His rest. Is it not also appropriate for us to fear that, if God has given us a promise of power in our personal lives and power in the corporate body of the church, we might come short of it?

The Promise of the Father

In Acts 1 we read that the disciples were with Jesus in Bethany, from where He would soon be departing from them and ascending into heaven. The clouds would receive Him out of their sight. He was giving to them their final instructions, which were of the utmost importance. In Acts 1:4 Jesus told them not to depart from Jerusalem, but to wait for the *promise* of the Father, which, He said, "You have heard of me." In Luke 24:49 Jesus said, "And, behold, I send the *promise* of my Father upon you; but tarry ye in the city of Jerusalem until ye be endued with power from on high."

In both places Jesus referred to the promise of the

Father, which is no doubt a reference to Joel 2:28,29, where God promised, "And it shall come to pass afterward that I will pour out my Spirit upon all flesh, and your sons and daughters shall prophesy, your old men shall dream dreams, your young men shall see visions; and also upon the servants and upon the handmaids in those days will I pour out my Spirit." This is confirmed in the second chapter of Acts, when the crowd that had assembled as a result of the supernatural phenomena accompanying the outpouring of the Holy Spirit was asking the question, "What does this mean?" Peter in explanation replied, "This is that which was spoken of by the prophet Joel," and he quoted the prophecy of Joel. The promise of God was that the day would come when He would pour out His Spirit, not just upon special individuals, but upon all flesh.

The Promise of the Savior

Jesus had also promised the Spirit to His disciples in John 14:16,17, where He said, "And I will pray the Father, and He shall give you another Comforter, that He may abide with you forever, even the Spirit of truth, whom the world cannot receive because it seeth Him not neither knoweth Him; but ye know Him, for He dwells with you and shall be in you." When Jesus promised the Holy Spirit, He referred to Him as "another Comforter." The word translated "comforter" comes from the Greek word *parakletos*, which literally means "to come alongside to help." This is the basic ministry of the Holy Spirit to the believer. He is there to help us. Up to this time Jesus had been alongside His disciples, helping them. They had rightly come to depend upon His help. He was the Master of every situation.

When the storm threatened to sink their little

boat, Jesus rebuked the winds and the waves, and there was a great calm. When the tax collector was demanding unjust taxes, Jesus told Peter to go down and catch a fish and take the coin out of its mouth and pay the taxes. No matter what situation arose, Jesus was always alongside to help.

Now He has told them that He is leaving them. He won't be with them as in times past. Their hearts must have been troubled by His words, and they were afraid to face the future without Him. So He promised that He would not leave them without help, that He would ask the Father, and He would send them another Comforter or Helper to abide with them forever: the Spirit of truth. For our Christian walk, we are completely dependent upon the help of the Holy Spirit. It is impossible to do any worthwhile Christian service apart from His help.

Waiting in Jerusalem

Because the words "tarry in Jerusalem" are used in Luke's Gospel, many Pentecostals have established "tarrying meetings" as the way by which the power of the Holy Spirit is to be received in the believer's life. It should be noted that the command was to "tarry in Jerusalem," so to be entirely Scriptural, the tarrying meetings should all be in Jerusalem!

It is obvious that Jesus was not establishing a universal method by which the Holy Spirit would be imparted to believers in all ages. He was only encouraging them to wait for just a few days in Jerusalem until He sent the Holy Spirit as a gift to the church. Once the Holy Spirit was given on the Day of Pentecost, it was never necessary to tarry for Him again, and we do not find in the book of Acts any tarrying meetings, nor are they advocated in the New Testament as the method by which the gift of the Holy Spirit is to be received.

Dynamic Power for You

In Acts 1:8 Jesus promised His disciples that they would receive power when the Holy Spirit had come upon them, and that through this power they would bear witness of Christ to the uttermost parts of the earth. The Greek word translated "power" is *dunamis.* Our English word "dynamic" comes directly from this word, and that describes what the Holy Spirit is to be in us—the dynamic by which we live and serve God. Without this dynamic the Christian life is impossible and service is fruitless. What glorious new dimensions the power of the Holy Spirit brings into the believer's life—the power to be and to do all that God wants!

It is not God's will that your life in Christ be dull and drab, or that your service be a chore. God intends that your walk with Him be full of joy. He wants you to have power and victory in your life. If your life in Christ is not dynamic and victorious, God has something more for you. The promise of the gift of the Holy Spirit is "to you and to your children and to all that are afar off, even as many as the Lord our God shall call."

4

The Work of the Spirit
In the Life of the Believer

What is the intended work of the Spirit in the life of the believer? As we have already noted in John 14, His name "Comforter" indicates His coming alongside us to help us. I have not found my Christian walk to be easy. I find that my flesh fights me all the way. With Peter, I too have often discovered that the spirit indeed is willing, but the flesh is weak. I understand what Paul was talking about in Galatians 5 as he spoke of the warfare between the flesh and the spirit. If God has help for me, I'm ready for it; I want all the help I can get! I never want to set limits on what God wants to give me, or what He wants to do in my life. I do not want to be guilty, as were the Israelites in the wilderness, of limiting God (Psalm 78:41). By the same token, I am not looking for experience for experience's sake; I want only the genuine work of the Holy Spirit, but I want it all.

Trusting the Spirit

In the discourse of Jesus to His disciples, beginning in John chapter 14, He is seeking to prepare them for His departure. He is talking much about His leaving them and returning to the Father. He also speaks much to them of the provisions which the Father and He had made for them by the power of the Holy Spirit. He would be there to help them. As they had learned to trust in Jesus for any situation or emergency that might arise, they must now learn to trust in the Holy Spirit. He will now be their Helper.

Jesus spent His three years with His disciples teaching them the truth of God. Now their Teacher is departing to return to the Father, but the students will not be on their own; this Helper, the Holy Spirit, will now teach them all things and will recall to their remembrance all the things that Jesus had said to them (John 14:26).

Perhaps you've had the experience of sharing the gospel with someone when he or she asked a question that immediately stumped you; but as you began to answer, the Scriptures started coming into your mind, and you were pleased and satisfied with the answer you gave the person. This is the *recall work* of the Spirit.

The Holy Spirit helps us to understand the things of God. Many times I have been frustrated in an attempt to explain some spiritual truth to a nonbeliever. It seems so clear and obviously evident, yet he or she cannot seem to grasp it. If you are dealing with things concerning the Spirit of God, the natural man "receives them not, neither can he know them, for they are spiritually discerned" (1 Corinthians 2:14).

Dead Versus Living Spirit

While attending college I had a sociology professor who believed in the dichotomy of man, and I believed in the trichotomy of man. Many times we expressed our differing views to each other. I was frustrated that he could make no distinction between the soul and spirit of man, but believed them to be synonymous. One day as I was leaving class frustrated after another discussion in which he seemed to have deliberate blindness, it was as though the Holy Spirit brought 1 Corinthians 2:14 to mind. Then I realized that as an unregenerate person his spirit was dead, so I was speaking to him of mysteries which he could not know. He did not and could not know of the spirit of man until he was born of the Holy Spirit. In 1 Corinthians 2:15 Paul says, "He that is spiritual understands all things, yet he himself is understood by no man."

Anyone who lives only on the body-conscious plane is living on the animal level of existence. His mind is ruled and dominated by his body needs; he does not understand the things of the Spirit, for his own spirit is dead. No wonder he seeks to relate himself to the animal kingdom, for he is living as an animal, a body-dominated consciousness. When a person is born again by the Spirit, his own spirit comes alive and, now joined to God by the Spirit, he is encouraged through the Word to live a Spirit-dominated life. As he does, he begins to have a Spirit-dominated consciousness.

Letting the Spirit Lead

As we live after the Spirit, our thought patterns are different because we are now thinking of God and how we might please Him and serve Him. The mind of the Spirit is life and peace (Romans 8:6). What a tremendous help the Holy Spirit is to us as He teaches us the things of God and helps us to understand them! The Bible seems to come alive with meaning and excitement as Scripture after Scripture seems to almost jump off the page to minister to us.

In John 16:13 Jesus promised His disciples that when the Spirit of truth had come He would guide them into all truth, and would show them things to come. It is so necessary to have that guidance of the Holy Spirit into all truth. Jesus warned of false prophets that would be wolves, yet appear in sheep's clothing (Matthew 7:15). There are men who come among the flock of God and appear to be part of it, but whose main motive is to prey upon the flock. They bring in damnable heresies and seek to draw men after themselves. In Acts 20:29,30 Paul warned the elders of the church in Ephesus, "For I know this, that after my departing shall grievous wolves enter in among you, not sparing the flock. Also of your own selves shall men arise, speaking perverse things, to draw away disciples after them."

Peter warns in 2 Peter 2:1-3, "But there were false prophets also among the people, even as there shall be false teachers among you, who privily shall bring in damnable heresies, even denying the Lord that bought them, and bring upon themselves swift destruction. And through covetousness shall they with feigned words make merchandise of you: whose judgment now of a long time lingereth not, and their damnation slumbereth not."

Sensing the Phony Prophets

Note one of the marks of the false prophet: "...with feigned words make merchandise of you." I regularly receive computer-typed letters from noted evangelists that fit Peter's description perfectly. These letters will say such things as, "Benny, God laid you on my heart this morning, and I have been in prayer for you. I just can't get you off my mind, Benny; is everything all right? Is there some special need that I can pray about? Please write me immediately, because I love you, Benny, and I want to help you! Incidentally, my ministry is in one of its greatest financial crises ever. We are going to have to close down some of our great works for God unless we get your help immediately. If you don't have 50 dollars to send me, maybe you could borrow it elsewhere and help me keep God's faith work going. Plant your seed of faith today. God will help you repay the loan you get. Your partner in faith."

My name is not Benny, but somehow that is the way it has gotten on their mailing lists. These types of deceitful letters seek only to make merchandise of the people, and on the authority of God's Word I do not hesitate to call their authors false prophets.

This is charismania in one of its most blatant forms and is practiced by most of the charismatic evangelists, especially those who emphasize divine healing. I always marvel that they can have such faith for my healing and so little faith for their own financial needs.

It is beautiful to see how the Spirit will warn you when someone starts to get off in his doctrine. Quite often you cannot pinpoint the error immediately, but you know that something isn't quite right. The Spirit has been given to the believer to guide him into all truth.

Learning Things to Come

The Holy Spirit also shows us things to come. When Daniel was seeking a fuller understanding of the time of the end and the things he had written, he was commanded to "shut up the words, and seal the book, even to the time of the end: many shall run to and fro, and knowledge shall be increased" (Daniel 12:4). As Daniel persisted in his questioning, again the Lord said, "Go thy way, Daniel, for the words are closed up and sealed till the time of the end. Many shall be purified, and made white, and tried; but the wicked shall do wickedly: and none of the wicked shall understand; but the wise shall understand" (Daniel 12:9,10).

It is by the help of the Holy Spirit that a clearer understanding of the coming again of Jesus Christ has been given to the church. Paul the Apostle was shown by the Spirit some of the things that were to come upon his life as he said to the elders of Ephesus in Acts 20:22,23: "And now, behold, I go bound in the spirit unto Jerusalem, not knowing the things that shall befall me there, save that the Holy Spirit witnesseth in every city, saying that bonds and afflictions await me." Later, as Paul continued his journey toward Jerusalem, Agabus the Prophet took Paul's belt, bound himself with it, and said, "Thus saith the Holy Spirit, So shall the Jews at Jerusalem bind the man that owneth this girdle, and shall deliver him into the hands of the Gentiles" (Acts 21:11). Here is a classic example of the Holy Spirit showing Paul the things that were to come into his life.

Another example from Paul's life of this work of the Spirit is found in Acts 27:21-24: "But after long abstinence Paul stood forth in the midst of them and said, Sirs, ye should have hearkened unto me and not have loosed from Crete and have gained this harm and loss. And now I exhort you to be of good cheer, for there shall be no loss of any man's life among you, but of the ship. For there stood by me this night the angel of God, whose I am, and whom I serve, saying, Fear not, Paul; thou must be brought before Caesar: and, lo, God hath given thee all them that sail with thee."

The Mighty Hand of God

In a small prayer group we decided to pray one for another; we had the person to be prayed over sit in a chair in the center of the group. When it was my turn to be prayed for, someone spoke a word of prophecy by the Holy Spirit declaring that God's hand of blessing was going to come upon my ministry in a great way, that the people would come to hear the Word in such numbers that there would not be room in the church to contain them. The prophecy went on to declare that I was being given a new name which meant shepherd, for the Lord was going to make me a shepherd of many flocks.

Up until this time I had been struggling for almost 17 years in the ministry with such limited success that I was contemplating leaving the ministry for some other type of work. The church I was then pastoring was running around 100 in attendance in spite of all our efforts to increase its size through giving free hamburgers to everyone who brought a friend to Sunday school. As these words were being spoken, I was in my heart much like the man upon whom the king leaned—who, when he heard Elisha's promise of God's bountiful provision to come upon the starving inhabitants of Samaria, said, "If God should open windows in heaven, could such a thing be?"

Fortunately, God was merciful to me, for my fate was not the same as his; I have both seen the fulfillment of the prophecy and have been able to partake of it as we see the greatly expanded church facility filled to overcapacity, not just once but three times on Sunday mornings, and as we minister by cassette tapes and videotapes to hundreds of Bible study groups all over the world.

Power to Conquer

The work of the Holy Spirit in your life if you are a believer is to give you the power to be a witness for Jesus Christ, to give you the power to be all that God wants you to be. One of the most frustrating things in the world is trying to live the Christian life in the energy of the flesh. The Bible speaks of the frustration in Romans 7, where Paul speaks of how, when he tried to keep the law of God and to do good, he found that "when I would do good, evil is present with me. And the good that I would I do not. And that which I would not I do. Oh wretched man that I am!" Paul describes in Galatians 5 how the flesh wars against the spirit and the spirit against the flesh, and how these two are contrary to each other. Jesus said to Peter, "Watch and pray, that ye enter not into temptation; the spirit indeed is willing, but the flesh is weak" (Matthew 26:41). Because of the weakness of our flesh, we cannot live the kind of life that the Lord would have us to live and that we ourselves would like to live before the world.

God desires that your life be a true representation of Him in this world. God wants the world to see Jesus Christ in you. He wants your actions and reactions to reflect Him. He wants you to be His witness, representing Him. But if you attempt to be His witness, if you try to react like Christ, you'll find how difficult and frustrating it is to do this—in fact, how *impossible* it is because of the weakness of the flesh.

The Perfect Witness

Many Christians find themselves in that frustration of knowing what is right and wanting what is right, but somehow not doing what is right. The Bible says of Jesus Christ that He was the true and faithful witness; He was a witness of the Father. If you want to know what God is like, just look at Jesus Christ, because He was the true and faithful Witness. When Philip cried out, "Lord, if You'll just show us the Father, we'll be satisfied," Jesus replied, "Have I been so long with you, and yet hast though not known me, Philip? He that hath seen me hath seen the Father; how sayest thou then, Show us the Father? Believest thou not that I am in the Father and the Father in me?... Believe me that I am in the Father and the Father in me, or else believe me for the very works' sake. Verily, verily, I say unto you, He that believeth on me, the works that I do shall he do also" (John 14:9-12). Jesus then gave the promise of the Holy Spirit to them.

Jesus faithfully represented God in every action. He demonstrated to us that God is interested in the physical, emotional, and spiritual welfare of man. God is interested in your sufferings; God is interested in your sorrows. God is interested in your pains; God is interested in your weaknesses. Jesus never came upon a sorrowing scene without bringing victory and joy to it. He never faced the weakness of humanity without imparting the strength of God.

The Great Helper

God wants to help you in your weakness, so He has sent another Comforter, one to come alongside you and help you. Jesus said, "Ye shall receive power when the Holy Ghost comes upon you." You will receive this dynamic. When I think of the power of the Holy Spirit, it is first the power to be what God wants me to be, and this extends into every area of my life: power in my prayer life, power for a holy walk, power to be and do. Here the promise is *power*, and it is related to being a witness for Jesus Christ: "Ye shall be witnesses."

We make a mistake when we think of witnessing as something we do; in reality it is something that we *are*. So often witnessing is associated with passing out tracts on the street corner, or going door to door to declare the gospel, or sharing the four spiritual laws with our neighbor over a cup of coffee. These are all forms of sharing our faith, but doing them does not make us witnesses of Jesus Christ. Being a witness is more than speaking words; it is living a life. The word "witness" comes from the Greek word *martus,* which transliterated into English is *martyr.* We think of a martyr as one who dies for his faith; however, it is really one whose life is so totally committed to his faith that nothing will dissuade him from it, not even the threat of death. His death does not make him a martyr; it only confirms that he was truly a martyr. Many Christians testify of Jesus Christ without ever being a true witness.

More Than Just Words

What a person *says* is often meaningless because he is not living a life that backs up what he is saying. If you are trying to share with someone the love that Jesus brings, yet your life is filled with hatred, bitterness, and jealousy, he will not respond to what you are saying because your life is contradicting what you are saying. If you go around saying, "You really need to know the joy of Jesus Christ; He'll give you such joy," but you're always depressed and pessimistic, your life isn't a witness of what you're saying. People will observe your depression and discount what you said. If you say, "You need to know the Lord so you can have real peace in your heart, the peace that passes all human understanding. Receive Jesus and have peace"—but your life is torn up and you're constantly nervous and worried and filled with anxiety, people will look at your anxiety and worry and won't hear what you're saying about peace. Your words can be totally drowned out by your actions. It is more important that the activities of your life be a witness for Jesus Christ, and then your words become meaningful. If your words aren't backed up by your life, your words really have no good effect at all.

A lot of people think, "I'm a witness for Jesus—I go down to the beach and pass out tracts. I share the four spiritual laws wherever I go." That doesn't make you a true and faithful witness. Your life must be in full harmony with God, so that when people look at your life they say, "There's something different about that person." *Saying* it doesn't make you a witness; *living* it does.

The Lord wants to give us the power to be a witness. He will empower us through the Holy Spirit, for in our own selves we are weak and failing. God wants us to be strong. God wants us as witnesses for Him.

Peter As a Failure

In Mark 14:53,54 we read, "And they led Jesus away to the high priest; and with Him were assembled all the chief priests and the elders and the scribes. And Peter followed him afar off, even into the palace of the high priest; and he sat with the servants, and warmed himself at the fire." As we follow the story through to verse 66 we read, "And as Peter was beneath in the palace, there cometh one of the maids of the high priest; and when she saw Peter warming himself, she looked upon him and said, 'And thou also wast with Jesus of Nazareth.' But he denied, saying, 'I know not, neither understand what thou sayest.' And he went out into the porch; and the cock crew. And a maid saw him again, and began to say to them that stood by, 'This is one of them.' And he denied it again. And a little later they that stood by said again to Peter, 'Surely thou art one of them, for thou art a Galilean, and thy speech agrees to this.' But he began to curse and swear, saying, 'I know not this man of whom ye speak.' And the second time the cock crew. And

Peter called to mind the word that Jesus said unto him: 'Before the cock crow twice thou shalt deny me thrice.' And when he thought thereon, he wept" (verses 66-72).

Earlier that evening Jesus had said, "All of you are going to be offended tonight because of me." But Peter had replied, "Lord, though they all be offended, I will never be offended." And Jesus had responded, "Peter, before the cock crows twice you will deny me three times." At this point Peter began to get very vehement, and he said, "Lord, even though they *slay me*, I would never deny You!"

Peter thought he was a true martyr, and I believe he was perfectly sincere. I know exactly how he felt when he made his boast to the Lord, for his spirit was willing and he really felt he had all it took to die for Jesus if necessary. But when the chips were down, Peter didn't have it; when this young maid asked, "Weren't you with Jesus?" Peter responded, "I don't know what you're talking about!" Later she said to a group standing there, "He is one of them," and Peter denied Jesus again. Then those standing by said, "Surely you are one of them; you have a Galilean accent." Then Peter began to curse and swear, saying, "I don't know the man!" Then came the reminder of what the Lord had predicted: the rooster began to crow. When Peter heard this he went out and wept. How many times I have wept over my own weakness and my own failure! I didn't want to fail the Lord; I didn't want to let Him down; I really wanted to stand for Him. But the pressure was too great, and I was not a witness—I failed. How bitter is that failure; how hard it is to realize, "Oh Lord, I failed You again." We get to the place where we don't even want to promise Him anything anymore, because we just know we'll fail Him again.

I can identify with Peter; I know exactly how he

felt when he heard that rooster crowing. I know exactly that misery—"Oh, God, I'm so sorry I failed You again." Must we go on forever in our Christian experience failing our Lord? No. Thank God we don't have to go on failing—He has promised to us the power to be what we could never be through our own strength or strong wishes.

Peter As a Witness

A few weeks later Peter faced the same group of men who had incited the murder of Jesus: "It came to pass on the morrow that their rulers, and elders, and scribes, and Annas the high priest, and Caiaphas, and John, and Alexander, and as many as were of the family of the high priest, were gathered together at Jerusalem. And when they had set them in the midst [that is, Peter and John and the lame man] they asked, 'By what power or what name have ye done this?' Then Peter, *filled with the Holy Spirit*, said unto them, 'Ye rulers of the people, and elders of Israel, if we this day be examined of the good deed done to the impotent man, by what means he is made whole, be it known unto you all, and to all the people of Israel, that by the name of Jesus Christ of Nazareth, whom ye crucified, whom God raised from the dead, even by Him doth this man stand here before you whole. This is the stone which was set at nought of you builders, which is become the head of the corner. Neither is there salvation in any other: for there is no other name under heaven given among men whereby we must be saved' " (Acts 4:5-12).

When they saw the boldness of Peter they marvelled (Acts 4:13). This is a different fellow from the one who a few weeks earlier stood on the porch of the palace and denied his Lord. What a different man! Reading the two accounts, you wouldn't believe it was the same person. What made the difference? The difference lies in that little phrase "filled with the Holy Spirit." Jesus had said to His disciples, "They are going to bring you before the magistrates and the judges, and when they do, do not worry about what you are going to say. Don't make any little prepared speeches, for in that hour the Holy Spirit will come upon you, and it will be the Holy Spirit who speaks through out. You shall receive power; you shall be witnesses." The Holy Spirit is the Helper, the One who helps you to be all that God wants you to be—a true and faithful witness of Him.

The Only Source of Power

The Holy Spirit gives us the power to be a true and faithful witness of Jesus Christ—the power of truly representing Him on the job, in the home, or in the classroom—so that when people look at us they will see the love, the peace, and the beauty of Jesus Christ in our actions and attitudes. They will see a person who is at peace in the storm. That is the power that we need if we are to be His witnesses, for we cannot be a true witness of Him in our own strength or ability; without the power of the Holy Spirit we will fail every time the real issue arises and the pressure is on. It is not until we learn to rely completely on the Holy Spirit that we experience this power.

One of our most common mistakes is that when we see an area of weakness in our life we immediately try to compensate for it and to correct it ourselves. We say, "I'm sorry, Lord; I'll never do that again. I promise you, Lord." We mean what we say, yet we do it again. The problem is that we are trying to correct the issue ourselves, thinking that somehow, if we will only work at it a little harder or try a different approach, we can change and correct the weaknesses of our own character and nature.

It is not until we are brought to the total desperation of the helplessness of ourselves, and give up and surrender, that we know the joy of *His* victory. It wasn't until Paul cried out, "Oh wretched man that I am!" that he recognized the truth about himself and no longer looked for "Who has another program that I can try?" "Who has another formula?" Paul gave up and cried out for a power outside himself: "Oh wretched man that I am! Who shall deliver me? I can't deliver myself." He gave up trying to deliver himself and he recognized that he was wretched.

Then he answered his own question: "Thanks be unto God that, through the promise of Jesus Christ and the power of the Holy Spirit, God has provided for my victory." As we move into Romans 8 we read all about the Spirit-led, Spirit-filled, Spirit-directed, Spirit-empowered life. Paul concludes the chapter by saying that we are "more than conquerors through Him who loved us."

What a different story from the defeat and sad despair of the weakness of the flesh in chapter 7! What a glorious cry of victory—"More than conquerors through Him who loved us. For I am persuaded that neither death, nor life, nor principalities, nor powers, nor things present, nor things to come, nor height, nor depth, nor any other creature, shall be able to separate us from the love of God, which is in Christ Jesus our Lord!" (Romans 8:37-39).

That glorious cry of victory is possible because of the empowering of the Spirit when I give myself up and turn myself over to God and receive that power, that dynamic from God. At this point I allow the Holy Spirit to do His work within my life, the work that God has designed for Him to do.

Not My Own Power

The effect of this is that I cannot stand up and boast to you about what a wonderful person I am or about the wonderful witness I am for my Lord or about the wonderful way I react in tough situations. All boasting is now in God's work through His Spirit. I am still a wretched man, but thank God I have been delivered from my wretchedness through the power of the Holy Spirit. When I face a pressured situation now, and things are pushing in on every side, thank God the pressure doesn't even build up anymore. It's almost like sitting on the outside and watching the Spirit work rather than being involved. All of a sudden I say, "Thank God! That's not me; that's not the way I react!"

A retired naval officer accepted Jesus as his Lord a while ago. He had a foul tongue, as many military people do. After he accepted the Lord he was really all-out for Jesus. When he was about six months old in the Lord, he was out in the backyard mowing the lawn with his power mower, whistling as he bubbled in the joy of the Lord. As he was busy mowing and not watching very closely, he went under a tree and a limb caught him right in the forehead and laid him on his back.

As he lay there on his back, all of a sudden he got excited. He went running into the house, grabbed his wife, and said, "Honey, guess what happened to me!" She looked at his bloodied face and asked, "What happened to you? What did you do?" He replied, "That's not what it is; it's what I *didn't* do! When it happened I didn't cuss! Not even one bad word!" She responded, "Honey, do you know that I haven't heard you use a bad word in six months?"

He asked, "You haven't?" The Lord had taken away his foul tongue without his even realizing it, until a situation came along that was so apt to arouse the old nature that suddenly he realized that God had given him the victory.

Changed on the Inside

That's the beautiful way of the Holy Spirit; He works in such a way that many times the work is already accomplished, and we don't even realize it. We're changed from within; that's the method of the Spirit. It's the change from within that comes out, which is exactly the opposite of the method by which we have been trying to do it. We have been trying to force the changes from the outside in. We can sometimes be successful in changing the outside, but if the inside isn't changed, what is *in* will eventually come *out*.

It is important that the Spirit do the changing from *within*. When this happens, only God can receive the glory. Where is my boasting? It is excluded. There is no way I can boast, because what I was I still am. But thanks be to God for His grace: through the power of His Holy Spirit I am now a new creature in Christ Jesus. The old nature I count as dead. Does this mean that I never get angry? No, I wish it did. But it does mean this: whenever I do get angry and fail, I say, "Lord, let Your Spirit work. Give me the power, Lord; I can't do it. You will have to do it, Lord; give me the power." In one area after another in my life, when I yield that area of weakness to the power of the Holy Spirit, I begin to experience real changes as the Spirit works within me and conforms me into the image of Christ.

Closing the Door?

In the Sermon on the Mount Jesus made a very

remarkable statement, one that must have puzzled those who heard it. In Matthew 5:20 He said, "For I say unto you that except your righteousness shall exceed the righteousness of the scribes and Pharisees, you shall in no case enter into the kingdom of heaven." It is our desire, goal, and prayer that we might enter into the kingdom of heaven. But it would seem that Jesus was actually closing rather than opening the door of the kingdom of heaven when He made this astounding statement, for the Pharisees practiced being righteous. They spent their lives trying to interpret the right action, then sought to do it. When Jesus said to His disciples, "Except your righteousness exceed that of the scribes and Pharisees, you shall in no wise enter the kingdom of heaven," I imagine that a sorrowful sigh went through them as they gave up hope of ever entering.

Then Jesus went on to close the door even tighter, because He began to give a series of illustrations to explain what He meant—illustrations of how the law was wrongly interpreted by the scribes and Pharisees. Then He contrasted that with how the law was originally meant to be understood. The basic flaw in the Pharisees' interpretation of the law was that they were interpreting it so they could fulfill it and feel good about it. They were interpreting the law to live comfortably with it—but you can't live comfortably with the law. They had begun to feel that they had fulfilled the law, and were going around doing their little righteous acts and thinking they were righteous.

But Jesus showed them that, though their actions were correct, their attitudes were wrong, and thus they were sinners, for the law was spiritual. The law wasn't intended to deal with just the outward actions of man; it was intended to deal with the *inner attitudes* of man. When the law says, "Thou shalt not murder," you can't really sit back comfortably and boast in yourself by saying, "Well, I've never killed anybody." If you feel smug and self-righteous that you have kept that law, remember that Jesus said, "The way God meant this is that you are not even to hate your brother." The attitude of hatred, Jesus said, was equivalent to the action of murder, as far as the violating of the law.

So it would seem that Jesus was closing the door to the kingdom of God. Finally we get to the last verse of Matthew 5, where it seems like He bolted and locked it, for there He said, "Be ye therefore perfect, even as your Father in heaven is perfect."

I Give Up!

All of a sudden I realize I cannot attain what God requires of me, because no matter how hard I try, I can't be perfect. I have failed, and there is no way I can fulfill God's requirement or the command of Jesus Christ. It's not that I don't want to be perfect. The Lord knows I'd love to be perfect, especially when I'm wrong. It would be nice to always do the right thing; it would be nice to always have the right reaction; but I don't. Many times I have a very wrong reaction to things, and that's when I wish I were right.

This is what psychologists call our superego—the picture of our ideal self, what we really want to be, and what we would be if circumstances were only different. In contrast to this is our actual self, our real self, our ego—that which we really are. Psychologists tell us that our mental problems are sometimes caused by the disparity between the two. If the real you is far removed from the ideal you, then you may have great mental conflicts. The closer together the ideal you and the real you are, the better-adjusted person you are.

If you go to a psychologist because you are mentally disturbed, he will attempt to discover what you really think you should be—the ideal you—and where in your actual self you are failing. Often he will then try to bring down your concept of the ideal you. He will seek to show you that your values are so high and pure that they are impractical. Often he will seek to lower your standards in order to remove your inner conflicts.

However, when the Lord works on us, He does the opposite. He tries to bring the real you closer to the ideal you. Man working on the problem would bring the ideal you down; the Lord working on the problem would bring the real you up to match the ideal. But God requires of us that which we cannot attain, that which we cannot give.

God's Provision

There is no way that I can fulfill the divine ideal for my life, so God, realizing that, has made provision for me. Knowing that I cannot attain to His divine ideal, God sent His only begotten Son to take all of my failures, all of my sin, all of my short-comings—and to accept the responsibility for them and to die in my place. God, knowing that I cannot fulfill the divine ideal, has inaugurated a substitute plan so that now what God requires of me is only that I believe in His Son, Jesus Christ.

I can do that! Though I cannot be perfect as God has *ideally* required of me, I can believe in Jesus Christ, which is God's *actual* requirement for me. You see, God has now made the kingdom of God open and available to all of us because all it takes is for us to believe in Jesus Christ. When people came to Jesus and asked, "What shall we do that we might work the works of God?" Jesus answered, "This is the work of God, that you believe on Him whom He hath sent." You cannot stand before God in that day of judgment and try to excuse yourself by saying, "Well, God, I just couldn't be perfect. I'm just human; I just had all these faults, and I just couldn't keep your requirements, so I just gave up because I figured there's no sense trying." God will reject your excuse because God has only required that you believe in Jesus Christ, the provision that He made for your failing and sinful self. God has made the kingdom of heaven available for everyone. You don't have to be perfect to get there. All you have to do is believe on God's provision through Jesus Christ.

But when you believe on Jesus Christ, and you open the door of your heart and invite Him to come in, then as the Spirit of God comes in He begins to work within you and change you. The Bible says, "If any man be in Christ, he is a new creation, and the old things are passed away, and behold all things become new." God's Spirit begins to work in your life to do in you what you couldn't do for yourself. God's Spirit begins His work of change in you, strengthening you, helping you, and conforming you into the image of Jesus Christ.

God's Ideal

As we look around us today and seek to understand God by His creation—God's purpose for man and what His intention was when He created man and placed him on the earth—we cannot discover this truth, for we do not see man fulfilling that ideal. The only place we can discover what God really intended man to be is in Jesus Christ. He is what God intended when in that divine council they said, "Let us make man in our image, after our own likeness."

What did God intend? Look at Jesus Christ and you'll know, for Jesus said, "I do always those things that please the Father." The Father said about Christ, "This is my beloved Son, in whom I am well pleased." As we look at Jesus Christ we see what God intended man to be. We cannot look at Adam, because

Adam fell, even though God did not intend for man to fall. We cannot look at ourselves, because we have fallen, even though God didn't intend for us to fall. But if we look at Jesus Christ, there we find the divine ideal, that which God intended when He created man. It is the purpose of God that, through the work of His Holy Spirit in your life, and through the power of the Spirit to bring about changes in you, He will bring you into the likeness or image of Jesus Christ.

In Ephesians 4:13 we see what God wants to do in us. Paul declares, "...till we all come in the unity of the faith and the knowledge of the Son of God unto a perfect man, unto the measure of the stature of the fullness of Christ." That's what God is working in us today. That's the work that God seeks to accomplish in our lives through His Holy Spirit, bringing us unto the perfect man, unto the measure of the stature of the fullness of Christ. In Romans 8:29 we read of the work of the Holy Spirit within us, conforming us into the image of God's Son. It is God's predestined purpose for us that He by the Holy Spirit might conform us into the image of His Son.

How It Works

In 2 Corinthians 3:6-18 Paul talks about the Old Testament period when God first gave the law. When Moses came down from the mountain having been there in the glory of God's presence, his face shone so that he had to put a veil over his face when he talked with the people (verse 13). But then in verse 18, in contrast to this veil, Paul said, "We all with unveiled faces, beholding as in a mirror the glory of the Lord, are changed into the same image from glory to glory, even as by the Spirit the Lord."

It is when I look at God's divine ideal in Jesus

Christ that the Holy Spirit works in me, changing me from glory to glory into the image of Christ. I believe that this is a lifelong work. The Holy Spirit has not completed His work in my life by a long shot. But, praise the Lord, He's working. And, praise the Lord, I'm not what I was—I'm being changed! Those changes are taking place, though I confess that they're taking place too slowly for my own desire. I would love to have them made all at once.

Whenever the Holy Spirit shows me an area that needs working on, whenever He opens up the light and causes me to see my true self and how far it is from what God would have me to be, immediately I think, "Oh, let's get to it; let's conquer." I step in and try to be better, and I keep trying to be better, but the harder I try the worse I get, until I get to the place of defeat and giving up. Then I cry out, "Oh God, I'm so wretched. I cannot do it." He replies, "Good. Now will you step aside and let me work? You've been in my way." He is not interested in my self-righteousness; He is not interested in my help. He wants to do His work in me unhindered by my fumbling efforts, because even if He used my fumbling efforts to help give me the victory, I'd be going around boasting in my fumbling rather than in my God. God lets me fail until in despair I cry out for help. As I yield myself to the Spirit of God and allow Him to do His work, He conforms me into the image of Jesus Christ.

I'm No Match

I must be brought to the place of acknowledgement and recognition that I cannot rid myself of the flesh or its desires or weaknesses. I'm no match. As long as I'm struggling and trying, I cannot make it; I will fail.

We're sinners; we need to recognize that fact;

there is nothing we can do about it ourselves. We have to call out for a power greater than our own. That's what Paul was doing in Romans 7 when he said, "Oh wretched man that I am! Who shall deliver me from the body of this death?" (verse 24). He called out for a power greater than himself, and when he did so, he found the power.

When we with open face behold the glory of the Lord we are changed from glory to glory. God is changing us—changing our attitudes. By our Adamic nature we are very selfish and self-centered. It begins very early in life; you can see it in small children as they say "mine"; it's one of the first words they learn outside of "mama" and "dada." You see them clutching their possession, and you don't dare try to take it away from them or you will hear about it in no uncertain terms. If you take their bottle away, you've got a fight on your hands—screaming, hollering, and kicking. It's just fortunate that they are as small and weak as they are, or they would tear the crib to pieces! They are blessed little children, but they have the Adamic nature.

As long as I am selfish and self-centered, I am not what God wants me to be. God does not want me to be self-centered. God does not want me to be interested in my own welfare first. The Lord wants me to be interested in other people and to share what I have with them in their need. That is what Jesus was talking about in Matthew 5 when He said, "Be ye therefore perfect; even as your Father in heaven is perfect." But this isn't natural; it's *supernatural*, and we can attain it only by the supernatural power of the Holy Spirit coming in and changing our attitude concerning ourselves and our possessions.

Not only does He change the attitude (which is the most important thing), but the changed attitude changes *action*. Too often we try to do it the other way around. It seems that our philosophy is to change a person's actions and hope that by changing his actions we can change his attitude. Psychologists say that if we act out emotion we will get the corresponding emotion. But God is interested in truly changing the attitude of our heart, and this changed attitude brings the changed action of our life.

The Change from Within

The gospel and the Holy Spirit work from the inside out. My heart is changed and my attitude is changed, and thus my actions reflect the changed attitudes within. The Holy Spirit working in me is changing me from glory to glory, bringing me into the image of Jesus Christ. How? By my looking at Him with unveiled face. How do I see Him? I can only see Him in the Word, and the Spirit makes the Word alive to my heart.

Peter tells us in his second epistle that God has given us exceedingly rich and precious promises, and that by these we are made partakers of the divine nature. It is there in the Book, but you must behold Jesus in the Book; you must look for Him there. Many people read the Bible with their faces veiled. It takes the Holy Spirit to open the Bible, to take the veil off their eyes so they can understand. The work of the Holy Spirit within us is so important. We cannot be what God would have us to be apart from the working of the Holy Spirit within our life.

No one knows me as well as I know myself except the Lord, and He knows me better than I know myself. A lot of things that I thought about myself I discovered were not true. Many of the things in my ideal self-image did not turn out like I thought they would. When I looked at myself through rose-colored glasses, I looked very rosy! But when the Holy Spirit broke my glasses, I was surprised. But He had to. He had to destroy my illusions of myself in order to deal with those areas of my life that I refused to acknowledge to Him. He had to bring them forth and reveal them in all of their ugliness so that He could then work to rid me of them.

A Son of God

I know that I am now a son of God, not through any righteousness of my own, but by my faith in Jesus Christ. "As many as received Him, to them gave He power to become the sons of God, even to those that believe on His name" (John 1:12). Because I believed on Jesus Christ, God gave me the power to become a son of God. So now I know I am a son of God, and that to me is absolutely glorious. If I am a son, then I am an heir. I am an heir of God and a joint-heir with Jesus Christ, and I do not know anything that could be more glorious than that.

God is working on my inner man by His Holy Spirit, but my problem is that though I am new on the inside, I am still the old Chuck on the outside. But the old Chuck is actually dead, so I have got to drag this old corpse around until the day that God finally delivers me from it. With my mind and with my heart I serve the Lord, but so many times with my body I am controlled by my own selfish desires. This old corpse gets heavy and hard to carry around. There are times when I groan, desiring to be delivered, not that I would be an unembodied spirit, but that I might be clothed upon with that new body which is from heaven, that I might be like Him, as I see Him as He is.

I am a son of God. I have a renewed spirit in an unredeemed body. God is not going to take this body into heaven, praise the Lord! "This corruption must put on incorruption." A change is starting to take place now: "We with open face beholding the glory of the Lord are *changed...*" This particular word *changed* in the Greek is *metamorphoo.* The word is used to describe a change of body, as when a caterpillar is changed into a butterfly. Paul said that all creation groans and travails together until now, waiting for the manifestation of the sons of God, namely, the redemption of our bodies.

Like Christ Forever

I should never be satisfied with myself or with my present state of development until I am like Jesus Christ. David said, "I shall be satisfied when I awake in Thy likeness." The morning I wake up and take a deep breath of air, and there is no smog, and I feel so different, and I realize that this corruption has put on incorruption—then I will be satisfied, for I will be like Him, for I will see Him as He is. That is what the Spirit is bringing me to; that is the purpose of the work of the Holy Spirit in my life. He will not be satisfied until He is finished and brings me into complete conformity to the image of Christ.

The final change will take place at the coming again of Jesus Christ for me, whether it be by death or the rapture of the church. At that time the old nature will be put off and the final change made, but I should not wait for that day. Even now, as I look to Jesus, the process of change is taking place. We should be closer to the image of Christ this year than we were last year, and next year than we are this year, for we grow in grace and in the knowledge of Him, and the Spirit working in us should be bringing us more and more into His likeness.

Mature or Just Old?

I love to be around saints who have been walking with the Lord for 50, 60, 70 years. I mean those who have really been developing in their walk. I know there are some who have been around 50, 60, 70 years but are still in their spiritual crib, and that is tragic. If you see a child that is just four or five months old, and his arms sort of wave excitedly, and he says, "Da da da..." you think, "That's beautiful; look how smart he is—what a beautiful child!" But if your child were 21 years old, and when you walked into the room he was lying on the bed and started smiling and saying, "Da da," it would no longer be a thrilling, exciting emotion—it would be very tragic.

That is the tragedy about so many people in the church today. After 15 or 20 years they are still at the same level of development. They are still banging their cribs. They have still got the same petty gripes. They are still upset with the message of last Sunday, and they are still divided in their little factions. They have not progressed at all. They are spiritual monstrosities because there has never been any development, and the problem is that there are so many of these Christians that it isn't even novel enough to be a curiosity. They are all over the place. They just have not delved into the Word of God to really behold the face of the Lord. They have not allowed the Word of God to really penetrate and the Spirit of God to really teach and instruct them in the things of the Lord or to reveal Jesus unto them in the Book.

How Far to Go?

Oh, that we would yield ourselves to the Holy Spirit now, that He might do His work in us, conforming us into the image of Jesus Christ! How far does He have to go in your life? Do you ever take one of these little self-evaluation tests to discover if you are appealing or a social bore? In 1 Corinthians 13 is a very simple little self-analysis test that you can take to find out how far the Spirit has come in your life in just one area: the area of love, one of the most important areas. Beginning with verse 4, the definition of this word "love" is given: "Love suffers long and is kind; love envies not, love vaunts not itself, is not puffed up, does not behave itself unseemly, seeks not its own, is not easily provoked, thinks no evil, rejoices not in iniquity, but rejoices in the truth; bears all things, believes all things, hopes all things, endures all things. Love never fails."

You say, "What's that got to do with me?" Take out the word "love" and put your name there instead. Then read the list again. "Chuck suffers long and is kind. Chuck envies not, Chuck vaunts not himself, is not puffed up, does not behave himself unseemly, seeks not his own, is not easily provoked, thinks no evil, etc." To the degree to which the text seems to be incongruous, to that degree I have failed from attaining what God wants me to attain. God help me to yield myself to the Holy Spirit so that He might do His work in me, so that what I have tried to do and failed—what I want but cannot achieve or attain—might be accomplished for me by His power.

5

The Agape Love of God

If a person did not make it to heaven he could blame a lot of people or circumstances, but there is one Person he will never be able to blame, and that is God. Someone might say, "It's the church's fault—I tried the church but it just didn't do anything for me." He might blame some poor example of Christianity that he saw: "Well, he said he was a Christian; but I saw the way he lived, and I decided I wanted nothing to do with that."

But one Person you can never blame is God. When I think of all that God has done to bring us salvation, I realize what a fight it is not to be saved. The Bible says, "If God is for us, who can be against us?" God so loved the world that He gave His only-begotten son, and then God sent His Spirit into the world to convict us of our sins and to draw us to Jesus Christ. He points out our own helplessness, and then points to Jesus Christ as the Answer—the Way, the Truth, and the Life.

Starting the Real Work

Once we have been brought to this point of coming to Jesus, and we say, "Okay, Lord, take over my life"—the moment we surrender ourselves to God—the Holy Spirit begins His work in us in earnest. The moment the door of our heart is open to receive salvation, the Holy Spirit comes into our life, and He begins to make those necessary changes within, conforming us into the image of Christ and empowering us to be the kind of person the Lord would have us to be. He gives us knowledge and understanding in the things of God, so that suddenly the Bible becomes a totally new book to us. As we start to read, it begins to come alive, because the Spirit begins to open up our understanding and fill our heart with God's *agape* love. But it first takes our coming to Jesus and submitting our life to Him.

Jesus said in Revelation 3:20, "Behold, I stand at the door and knock; if any man hear my voice and open the door, I will come in to him and will sup with him, and he with me." It actually means "eat supper with him." In the Orient, the greatest method of communion with a person was to eat with him. In eating together with a person, you have created a unity or a bond. Since you have partaken of the same food, it now becomes part of both of you, and so you become part of each other. The people of the Orient placed great significance on the breaking of bread together and the drinking from the same cup, because it created an affinity, a unity. It is interesting to note that Jesus always liked to eat supper with people. He enjoyed that oneness, that identity with people.

It is significant that Jesus says, "I'm standing at the door knocking; if you will open the door, I will come in and eat supper with you." He will come into your life and you can begin that beautiful, intimate relationship with Him in which you become a part of each other. This is all done through the work of the Holy Spirit. The moment I open the door and believe on Jesus, the Spirit does a marvelous work for me and in me. In Ephesians 1:13 and following, we read about this work of the Holy Spirit in sealing the believer. Paul describes for us all the fantastic blessings that we have as children of God. He begins in 1:3 by saying, "Blessed be the God and Father of our Lord Jesus Christ, who has blessed us with all spiritual blessings." Then he begins to list some of those glorious blessings with which God has blessed us.

Blessed Beyond Description

The Christian is actually the most blessed person in the world. God has just blessed us until we cannot take any more. And after He is all through blessing us here, He is going to receive us into the eternal glory, where He is going to bless us forever. Paul talks about the blessings of God: He has chosen us, predestined us, accepted us, redeemed us, forgiven us, made known to us the mystery of His will, and given us an inheritance. In Ephesians 1:13 Paul says, "...in whom ye also trusted after ye heard the word of truth, the gospel of your salvation; in whom also after you believed...."

It all begins with hearing "the word of truth, the gospel of your salvation." Paul said, "How can they believe on Him whom they have not heard?" It is necessary for faith that you first hear the message that God loves you with an everlasting love, and that because He loves you He sent His Son to take your sin and die in your place, so that which kept you from God could be put aside and nothing would hinder your fellowship with God.

God said through the Prophet Isaiah, "The Lord's hand is not shortened that He cannot save; neither is His ear heavy that He cannot hear, but your sins have separated between you and your God" (Isaiah 59:1,2). That is always the tragic by-product of sin—separation from God. Sin in my life separates me from God. God did not want that separation, but sin had to be dealt with, so God sent His Son to take my sins—to die in my place—so that I would not have to be separated, and could come back into fellowship with God.

If you are born again, you heard God's good news for you, and you trusted after you heard. First there was the *hearing* and then the *believing* of what God said. Then, after you believed, after you opened the door, you were "sealed with that Holy Spirit of promise."

God's Seal of Ownership

The seal was used in ancient days primarily as a stamp of ownership. The city of Ephesus was a major port where goods from Asia were brought and then shipped to other places, including Rome. The merchants from Rome would come to Ephesus to buy their goods there. Then they would seal those goods with their signet ring in wax. When the ship arrived at Puteoli (the port where they would land the goods going to Rome), the merchant would claim his goods, proving his ownership by his own personal seal. If someone else started to claim the goods, the merchant could say, "Those are mine. That's my stamp of ownership."

The beautiful Biblical truth is that, once I believed, God sealed me with His own personal stamp of ownership. He actually claimed me as His own possession, so that when the enemy would try to claim me, God would say, "Keep your hands off— he's mine!" That seal of God's ownership is the Holy Spirit. When you believe in Jesus Christ, the Holy Spirit comes into your life, and the indwelling of the Holy Spirit in your life is God's seal, God's mark of ownership by which He claims you as His own.

Treasured by God

I do not understand why God prizes me so highly, but He does. In Ephesians 1:18 Paul says, "...that ye may know what is the hope of His calling, and what the riches of the glory of His inheritance in the saints." He's saying, in other words, "May God open up your eyes to realize how much He treasures you!" I pray that God would open my eyes by the Spirit so that I might find how much God treasures me. That to me is glorious—that God would treasure me.

For His own reasons God treasures us, and He has placed His seal on us. The Holy Spirit within us is God's seal. We are also told this in 2 Corinthians 1:22: "...who hath also sealed us and given the earnest of the Spirit in our hearts." In Ephesians 4:30 we are commanded, "Grieve not the Holy Spirit of God, by whom ye are sealed unto the day of redemption."

The Future Claim

God has put his stamp of ownership on you at this point because He is claiming you as His own, even though your redemption is not yet complete. That is why the merchants put their stamp of ownership on their merchandise—because they had not yet claimed their goods in the home port. So wherever these goods went they were marked; they had the seal of ownership. In the same way God has put His seal of ownership on you, though He has not yet claimed His purchased possession. Our redemption is not yet complete, but the Holy Spirit is that seal and "the earnest."

In Ephesians 1:14 Paul declares, "...which is the earnest of our inheritance until the redemption of the purchased possession, unto the praise of His glory." The Holy Spirit is not only the *seal* of God's ownership, but He is also the *earnest*, which means a deposit or down payment. God has every intention of completing your redemption. He has made the deposit or down payment—the Holy Spirit. God is declaring His intention of completing His transaction for you.

This redemption will not be complete until we are freed from this body. This body is the thing that is still dragging us down. Paul said, "We who are in this body do groan." In Romans 8:22 he describes how we "groan and travail." All of creation is actually groaning and travailing together until now. Romans 8:23 says, "and not only they but ourselves also, who have the firstfruits of the Spirit, even we ourselves groan within ourselves, waiting for the adoption [literally being placed as sons], the redemption of our body."

The End of the Old Body

Robert Service, in his poem "The Cremation of Sam Magee," speaks of hurrying on "with a corpse half hid that he couldn't get rid...." It was lashed to the sleigh, but he couldn't get rid of it because he had made this promise on Christmas Eve. That is the way we Christians are. We have a redeemed spirit which is alive unto God, but we have to carry around this old corpse of our body. It hangs on wherever we go, until someday we finally get rid of our load. Paul said, "We who are in this body do groan, earnestly desiring to be delivered, not that we would be unclothed, but that we might be clothed with that body which is from heaven." (See 2 Corinthians 5:1-4.) That will be the completion of our redemption. That is what I am waiting for.

Some people are troubled to think they are going to get rid of this body. It doesn't trouble me. The Apostle Paul said, "We know that when the earthly body of this tent is dissolved, we have a building of God not made with hands, eternal in the heavens." This body that I now possess has been passed down to me through my ancestry; all the gene factors have been passed down the line, so I am a composite of my ancestry. I have picked up all the inherited characteristics of man's failure, and so here I am in my groaning body.

The New Body from Heaven

The new body that I am going to have will not be passed down through failing man; it will be given to me directly from God. It is not going to be subject to pain or fatigue or gimpy football knees or so many of the other things I have experienced in this body. It is going to be coming to me directly from God. Paul calls this present body a "tent" in 2 Corinthians 5:4. You never think of a tent as a permanent place to live. If you have to live in a tent, it is all right for a few weeks in the mountains on vacation, but you do not like to think of it as a permanent place to live. It is so much better to move out of the tent into a real house. God is planning to redeem us completely.

The redemption includes not just a *redeemed* body, but a *new* body. With my mind I want to do the will of God. With my mind I want to turn it all over to God. Completely and fully I want to live the kind of life that God wants me to live. There is no problem with my heart and my mind. My problem is that my *body* keeps dragging me down. It keeps pulling me back and pulling me down, so that I do not always do those things that I want to do. I am pulled down by my body appetites. I cannot be all that I want to be, so I groan. All creation around us is groaning, waiting for the day of redemption, when God lays claim to that which is His. He has His stamp of ownership on it, and one day He is going to come down and say, "This is it." He is going to release my soul and spirit from my body and immediately incorporate it into that new body which is from heaven.

The Suffering World

The same is true of this world. Right now the whole world is suffering as the result of sin: "All creation groans and travails." Every thorn, they say, is an undeveloped blossom. Thorns have come as a result of the curse. And a thorn is just a mark of groaning creation—wanting to blossom out, but unable to. All creation suffers under the curse of sin, waiting for that day of deliverance, waiting for that day when God redeems what He has purchased.

Jesus purchased the world, but He has not yet claimed it. It belongs to Him, but He has not claimed it. It is still under Satan's control. But one of these days very soon He will come back to claim what he purchased. We read about this in Revelation chapter 5. There is a scroll in the right hand of Him who sits upon the throne. An angel declares in a loud voice, "Who is worthy to take the scroll and loose the seals?" John responds, "I began to weep because no one was found worthy." The elder replies, "Don't weep, John; the Lion of the tribe of Judah has prevailed to take the scroll and to loose its seals." So John says, "I turned and saw Him like a lamb that had been slaughtered, and He took the scroll out of the right hand of Him who sits upon the throne." This scroll is the title deed to the earth. Who is worthy to take it? Who is worthy to claim it? No one but Jesus, for He purchased it on the cross, and He is coming back to lay claim to His purchased possession. And *I* am His purchased possession!

My Assurance

The work of the Holy Spirit today in my life is that

of having sealed me. So His indwelling gives me real assurance. When Satan comes and begins to badger me because of the weakness of my flesh and my failures, and begins to tell me that God is not interested in me and God does not love me and is not going to save me, I say, "Satan, you are *wrong!* I have God's seal; he has marked me; He has stamped me with His seal of ownership. The Holy Spirit indwells me. God has sealed me! He has given me the deposit, and He is coming to claim what He has redeemed."

When we get to heaven (either when Jesus comes for us at the rapture or when we die), we will have our redemption complete. The work of Christ will be finished in us, and we will share forever in the glorious kingdom of God without any further hindrances of this body. We will be able to love, to share, to give, and to relate with one another without any restrictions or limitations.

What a glorious day! What a glorious work of God in sealing us and giving us the earnest of the Spirit until that day of the redemption of the purchased possession!

The Agape Love of Christ

Another work of the Holy Spirit in the life of the believer is to bring us the agape love of Jesus Christ. Jesus said to His disciples, "By this sign shall men know that ye are my disciples: that ye *love* one another." The word translated "love" is the Greek word *agape,* which is rarely found in Greek outside the Bible. It is a word that was used by our Lord Jesus Christ to define a quality of love above an ordinary experience of love. The English language is restricted in some ways, and perhaps most limited in its ability to express love. The French say, "You Englishmen have one way to tell a woman you love her. We have a hundred." They are expressing how much freer and fuller the French language is than the English language in this respect. Within the Greek language are several words for love, but we are limited to just the word "love" in English. I *love* peanuts. I *love* CrackerJacks, and I *love* my wife. I have to use the same word to describe my feelings for hot fudge sundaes as my feelings for my children. Yet what I feel toward hot fudge sundaes is entirely different from what I feel toward my children or my wife. I am stuck with the one word "love."

Love's Three Words

In the Greek language there is a word for love on the physical plane—the word *eros*. It is easy to see the English words that we get from this Greek word, such as "erotic." It is love on the purely physical plane. This word has become vogue among young people today, and I guess older people, too. They say, "Let's make love," and by this they are referring to an eros experience, which does not necessarily involve true love at all.

The Greeks have a second word for love, a love on a higher plane than the physical—the mental plane, an emotional relationship. The word is *phileo*. This is far deeper than eros, because this involves deeper interaction with another person. Phileo is developed by conversing and finding out that we like the same things. We have a lot in common; we appreciate each other, and through a mutual sharing we come into the phileo experience of love.

Agape love is total love. It is love in the deepest area; it is true spiritual love. Eros is not true love. If I say "I love you" in the eros realm, what I am really saying is "I love *me*, and I want you because I'm in love with me, and I need you." If someone says, "I can't live without you," that does not express deep love for you—it only shows that he is thinking of himself. Eros is extremely selfish. It is self-love.

Phileo love is reciprocal: "I love you because you love me; I love you because you laugh at my jokes; I love you because we like so many of the same things; I love you because we get along well together and have a lot of fun when we're together. I love you because you love me, and you're a pleasant person, and we have a great time together."

The Highest Love

Agape love remains loving even if there is not a return of love. It is a deep love that gives and asks nothing in return. The love is so deep and so great that it just keeps on giving. In fact, that is the chief concern of agape: giving. The word *agape* is such a vast, broad word that it is difficult for us to even define it in the English language. It is impossible for us to understand it apart from the Spirit of God and His revelation to our heart, because it is not a natural love; it is a supernatural love. The Bible says, "God is *agape*." It is a divine, supernatural love, and it is probably best defined for us in 1 Corinthians 13.

First of all, Paul points out the supremacy of this agape love. It is more important that you have this kind of love than that you have spiritual gifts. Paul said, "Though I am able to speak with the tongues of man and angels...but have not this love (agape), I am become a sounding brass or a clanging cymbal." You may have very powerful oratory; you may have a silver tongue; you may be able to express yourself extremely well. But if you do not have agape love, it is no more meaningful than just clanging on a cymbal. It is a meaningless sound.

Agape is more important than the gifts of prophecy or the word of knowledge or the gift of faith, for "though I could prophecy and understand all things, and though I had all knowledge and faith so that I could remove mountains, if I have not agape, I am nothing." Paul continues, "and though I bestow all my goods to feed the poor..." agape love is even more important than sacrifice. You may sell everything you have and feed the poor, and give your body to be burned, making the supreme sacrifice, but if you do not have agape love, it profits you nothing.

Now Paul goes on to define this kind of love. "Love suffers long and is kind." This means that agape love receives abuse and suffers long. It takes and takes and at the end of the taking is still kind. You have heard people say, "All right, I've taken and taken, and that's it; now I'm going to get even." That is not agape. Agape takes and takes and then is still kind. It is not crying for vengeance. "Love envies not. It vaunts not itself and is not puffed up. It does not behave itself unseemly, does not seek its own [does not insist on its own way], is not provoked." (The word "easily" was inserted by the translators. They could not quite understand "is not provoked.") "Love thinks no evil; it rejoices not in iniquity but in the truth; love bears all things, believes all things, hopes all things, endures all things." Agape love "never fails."

Love's Two Signs

Jesus said, "By this sign shall men know that ye are my disciples, because ye love [agape] one another." This really becomes the most powerful evidence to the world that we are the disciples of our Lord Jesus Christ. This agape love should be working within our lives and making us one with each other, giving preference to one another, not exalting ourselves or forming cliques, but just sharing that oneness of love that makes us all one together. We should share together with one another the goodness and grace of God, freely giving as we have freely received of God's love and grace. As this agape love works within our lives, it becomes the sign to the world that we are truly Christ's disciples.

In 1 John 3:14 we read, "We know that we have passed from death unto life because we *love* the brethren." Again, the word *agape* is used. Not only is it a sign to the *world* that we are Christ's disciples, but it is a sign to *us* that we have passed from death to life. As God's love begins to work in my life, it becomes a sign to *me* that I have passed from death to life, because I have this love for the brethren, for those within the body of Christ.

The Source of True Love

Because this is a divine love, its source is in God. It is not something I can generate. It is not something I can work up within myself. This has been one of the difficulties within the Christian community—knowing that we are to love all believers, but also knowing that there are those whom we do not truly love. So we try to work up an artificial love. We try to talk ourselves into it. But agape love does not originate with me; agape's origin is in God. God is agape. I cannot develop it; it is something that has to come to me as a work of God within my life. If I find that I am lacking in this love, I cannot really do anything about it myself; I must just confess this lack to God and ask Him to plant that agape within me.

Many Christians have been totally frustrated because they have tried to produce this agape. They have sought so hard to love with this divine love, but they cannot do it. Its origin is in God, and it has to come from God as a gift to you, and then it goes forth from your life. If you find yourself lacking in this agape, the only thing you can do is to ask God to fill your heart with agape through the Holy Spirit. Do not browbeat yourself and become defeated in your spiritual walk because you find that you do not have this agape as you should; just ask the Lord for it.

6

The Word of God
Becomes Real

As we have been considering the work of the Holy Spirit in the life of the believer, we have seen how He gives us the power to be all that God would have us to be. Next we saw how He conforms us into the image of Jesus Christ: "We, with open faces beholding the glory of the Lord, are changed from glory to glory, even into this same image by His Spirit working in us." Next we saw how He brings to us the agape love of God, helping us receive it and then giving us the capacity to love with God's agape love, for the Holy Spirit has shed the love of God abroad in our hearts and in our lives.

Now we would like to study the work of the Holy Spirit in the life of the believer, making the things of God and the Word of God real to us.

Eye Has Not Seen

In 1 Corinthians 2:9 Paul wrote, "Eye has not seen, nor ear heard, neither have entered into the heart of man the things that God has prepared for those that love Him." This Scripture has often been misinterpreted. In fact, I think that of all the Scriptures in the Bible that have been misinterpreted or quoted out of context, this verse ranks near the top. You usually hear this Scripture quoted in regard to heaven. Heaven, we are told, is going to be so glorious, so marvelous, so beautiful that "eye has not seen, nor ear heard, neither have entered into the heart of man, the things that God has prepared for those that love Him."

All the time in church as I was growing up, this is the way I heard this passage quoted, and so the first ten years in my ministry I interpreted it like this too. Then one day I read the whole context and realized that Paul was not talking about heaven. Paul was talking about the things that God has for His people *right now*—those things that God has for us because He loves us and we love Him. What is Paul saying? The natural man cannot see, he cannot know, he cannot understand those things that God has for *us*. That is what he is talking about. The natural man's eye cannot see, his ear cannot hear, and neither has it entered into his heart those things that God has for *us* because we love Him. Peter tells us that even the angels desire to look into the things that God has in store for His church. It no doubt amazes them that God would actually come and dwell within us.

Notice what the next verse says: "But God *has* revealed them unto *us.*" Paul is not talking about heaven. He is talking about *the present glories of the life empowered by the Holy Spirit.* "God has revealed them unto us by His Spirit; for the Spirit searches all things, yea, the deep things of God. For what man knows the things of a man except the spirit of man which is in him?" (1 Corinthians 2:10,11). In other words, who really knows what is in your heart except you? You may be putting on a pretty good front; it could be that you are deceiving a lot of people. I really do not know what is in your heart. *You* know. You know what is covered and veiled and what you are hiding from everybody else. So, Paul is saying, "What man knows the things of a man except the spirit of man which is in him? Even so the things of God knows no man, but the Spirit of God" (1 Corinthians 2:11).

The Revealing Spirit

There are things that God knows (for example, aspects of God's love) that man just does not understand; only the Spirit of God understands these things. Paul continues, "We have received not the spirit of the world, but the Spirit which is of God, that we might know the things that are freely given to us of God" (1 Corinthians 2:12). The Holy Spirit lets us know those things that God has freely given to us. "Which things," Paul says, "we also speak, not in words which man's wisdom teaches, but which the Holy Spirit teaches, comparing spiritual things with spiritual. But the natural man receives not the things of the Spirit, for they are foolishness unto him; neither can he know them, because they are spiritually discerned" (1 Corinthians 2:13,14).

A lot of people have made the mistake of trying to discover what the Bible is all about on their own. They have read the Bible to discover its message, but they did it with only their human intellect. This usually ends in failure. They try to read, but they get nowhere. They say, "I've tried reading the Bible, but I can't see what anybody gets out of it. I just can't understand it." That's exactly what Paul is saying: "The natural man *cannot* understand the things of the Spirit, neither can he know them." It is *impossible* for the natural man or the natural mind to comprehend the things of the Spirit because he lacks the capacity to do so. You could say with equal logic that a blind man cannot appreciate the beauty of the sunset or a deaf man cannot enjoy the music of a concert, because he lacks the capacity by which these things are appreciated and understood. Unless the Holy Spirit opens our heart and our mind to these things, we just cannot understand them.

Seeing and Not Seeing

One of the most difficult things is to have a clear understanding of an issue and wonder why someone else does not have the same clear understanding. It is so plain! It is so obvious! Why can't you see it? It is right there—look! But if they are not spiritually awakened, if the Spirit of God is not dwelling in them, they can look all day and still not see it.

This understanding and this enlightenment must come through the power of the Holy Spirit to open up the things of God to our hearts. Paul prayed for the Ephesian believers in 1:17 that God might give to them the Spirit of wisdom and revelation in the knowledge of Him. The work of the Holy Spirit is to let us know that glorious grace of God bestowed unto us, that work of God in our behalf and that which God wants to do within our lives. How tragic it is that people are seeking to live the Christian life and to understand the Christian walk without the help of the Holy Spirit! It simply cannot be done.

God has made available unto us all that is necessary for life and godliness. God has not left a single thing out; no matter what the situation is that we might be facing, God has the way out for us. God has already made His provision. The Holy Spirit makes us aware of those things that God has already freely given us, so that we can then appropriate the work of God for our particular need and situation.

I do not sit down to read the Word of God without first saying, "Oh Holy Spirit, open my mind and my heart to receive and understand the Word of God." I dare not approach the Word of God with my own natural intellect. It will just be a blur. I need the help of the Holy Spirit to teach me what God has said. In 1 John 2:27 we read, "You have no need that any man should teach you, but that anointing which you have received shall teach you." So we can look to the Holy Spirit to teach and guide us as we study the Word of God.

Learning of Jesus

When we are talking with people who have just committed their lives to Jesus Christ, we seek to emphasize the importance of learning about Jesus. Jesus said three things: First, "Come unto me"; next, "Take my yoke upon you"; and then, "Learn of me." Salvation is more than just coming to Christ: it is taking His yoke upon us; it is submitting our lives to the mastery of Jesus Christ; it is turning the reins of our life over to Him. But then if I am to grow, I must learn of Him.

Many a person has failed to continue in the grace of God because he has not learned of Jesus Christ; he has not grown in his knowledge of Him. There is only one way you can learn of Jesus Christ, and that is by reading the Word of God. The Word of God is the only spiritual food for the new Christian, the spiritual babe; you cannot grow apart from the Word of God and the knowledge of God and Jesus Christ through the Word. It is vital for your Christian experience and for your Christian growth.

Which Way Is Right?

I am always instructing people, "Before you start to read, just pray, 'Lord, open my eyes and let me see, open my ears and let me hear what the Spirit would have to say through the Word.' " Some people say, "There are so many interpretations that I just get confused." I am not asking you to read some man's interpretation of the Bible. Just read the Bible itself. Some people ask, "How do you know your way is right? Maybe Joe Smith was right, or maybe the Jehovah's Witnesses are right, or maybe Mary Baker Eddy was right. Everyone has his own interpretation. How do you know you're right?" Let me say this: I am not at all worried what you will come to believe by just reading the Bible. I believe that the Holy Spirit is able to teach you—right out of the Bible itself—all that you need to know. I do not encourage you to read some interpretation of man. I encourage you to just read the Bible and let the Holy Spirit teach you what God has said.

I am not worried about how you are going to interpret the Bible if you just read the Bible alone. I am not worried about you getting off into some false doctrine or some weird trip if you are just reading the Bible. I *am* worried about the weird trips that you get on when you read some of the junk that is going around supposedly interpreting the Bible.

Learning and Recalling

Jesus said, "The Holy Spirit will come alongside you and help you; He will teach you all things and then bring all things to your remembrance, whatever I have commanded you." Notice that He will bring all things to your *remembrance*. What does that mean? This means that the things have to be planted there in order to be brought to remembrance. He cannot bring something to your remembrance that has not been planted in your mind first. It is important that you read the Word of God. David said, "Thy Word, O Lord, have I hid in my heart, that I might not sin against Thee." You may not remember what you read five minutes after you read it, yet a crisis situation may arise in your life and all of a sudden a Scripture pops into your mind.

What has happened? The Holy Spirit has brought to your remembrance that which had been placed there, and now in this moment of emergency the Holy Spirit has helped you.

In John 16 Jesus was talking with His disciples just before going to the Garden of Gethsemane, where He was to be arrested. This was the last night that Jesus was sharing with His disciples before His crucifixion. He said to them in verse 12, "I have yet many things to say unto you, but ye cannot bear them now." He had been with them for 3½ years teaching them, and now there were many things that He still had to say to them, but they were not capable of receiving them. So He said, "When He, the Spirit of truth, is come, He will guide you into all truth; for He shall not speak of Himself, but whatever He shall hear, that shall He speak; and he will show you things to come" (John 16:13). Jesus was saying, "I have a lot of things to say to you; you can't handle them now, but when the Spirit of truth is come, He will lead you into all truth, and He will show you things to come." The Spirit of God is given to us to teach us the things of God; the Spirit of God is given to us to lead us into the truth of God, and then to show us things that are going to come.

Knowing What's Coming

Concerning His showing us things to come, the Apostle Paul said in writing to the Thessalonian church, "Ye are not the children of darkness that that day [that is, the day of the Lord, the rapture of the church] should overtake you as a thief, but ye are children of the light; therefore walk as children of the light." What is he saying? He is saying that the day of the Lord, the coming of Christ for His church, should not take us by surprise. It should not catch us unawares. If we are walking in the Spirit, if we are being led by the Spirit, He is showing us things to come and is keeping us alert as to the day in which we live.

I am really shocked at how blind many people are to this age in which we live. I was on a radio-show panel one night in Los Angeles when I mentioned the second coming of Jesus Christ—His soon return. All the other panel members (who were religious leaders) thought that it was horrible to think that the Lord is coming soon, and that we ought to be more interested in making this a better world. I replied, "You've been trying to do that for a long time, but we're in the worst mess ever." I am surprised that they are not discouraged; you have to credit them for that! When you try so hard to make a better world but it just gets worse and worse, if you are not discouraged by now, you have got some kind of grit. But I think a person has to be totally blind to look around today and say, "How lovely! Things are getting better!"

They are not facing reality. I am a realist. The church, in its endeavor to make the world a better place to live, has just about wiped itself out. The methods by which they are seeking to make the world a better place to live are things I do not understand. When some church groups support African terrorist organizations and the PLO, I hardly see how this can contribute to a better world.

The Tragedy of Blindness

The frustrating thing about walking and being led by the Spirit is that when the Spirit shows you things that are so obvious and plain, you just cannot understand why the next fellow cannot see them. But the reason he cannot see them is because the natural man cannot understand the things of the Spirit: "...neither can he know them, for they are spiritually discerned." There are those who are such obvious counterfeits, yet people are deceived by them. It is like seeing the portrait of a *smiling* Abraham Lincoln on a five-dollar bill; it is so obvious that it is phony, and yet people are just as blindly duped and taken in. You think, "Can't you see? They're ripping you off! He's a phony." But they do not have the gift of discernment, and thus they are totally fooled. It is the hardest thing to see so clearly and not to understand why other people cannot see the issues as clearly as you can.

The return of Jesus Christ is so near; we are right at the end of the times of the Gentiles, and it is so obvious that the coming of the Lord is at hand. The Scriptures are so clearly fulfilled, and yet people are totally oblivious to this whole prophetic picture; they are blinded and continuing their lives as if they are going to be here forever. Unless the Holy Spirit had revealed the second coming to us, we would never have known it.

The Real Source of Truth

When John said, "You have need that no man should teach you, but the anointing which you have received will teach you all things," does this mean that I am not to fellowship at church, but to stay home and read my Bible, allowing the Holy Spirit to teach me there? No. Paul tells us that the Holy Spirit has placed pastors and teachers in the church for the perfecting of the saints for the work of the ministry. But the truth still stands that only the Holy Spirit can teach *you*, and if you receive any truth at all from God, you receive it only because the Holy Spirit has made it true and brought it to you, opening your heart to understand it. I might be bringing God's truth to you, and all of a sudden you say, "I see it! Oh, thank you, Chuck!" No, do not thank me, because you would never have seen it unless the Holy Spirit had revealed it to you.

Another person reading the same page did not catch it. He is still in as much darkness as he ever was. He does not understand it all; it went right over him. "Well, why did I see it and he didn't?" Because the Holy Spirit taught you the truth; you were ready for it. It was time for you to know, and the Holy Spirit opened your heart and taught you the truth. I perhaps declared the truth, but you cannot receive it or understand it unless the Holy Spirit brings it to you. Your understanding of spiritual things can only come through the Holy Spirit.

Two Kinds of Teachers

It also follows that you cannot teach the truth of God except by the Holy Spirit, for how can you teach that which you do not understand? This means that, though a man may know Greek and Hebrew fluently, and though he may have committed the Old and New Testaments to memory in the original languages, and though he may know all the commentaries, if he is not filled with the Spirit, he cannot be a true guide to you in the things of God. You would do better to listen to some young man without a seminary degree who is filled with the Spirit. An uneducated but Spirit-filled servant of God is a truer guide to Scriptural truths than a Ph.D. who is not born again, because no man can truly understand the things of the Spirit except the Spirit teach him, and no man can truly teach the things of the Spirit except the Spirit anoint him to teach.

Knowing the Greek language is very beneficial to understanding the New Testament, but the fact remains that it is the work of the *Holy Spirit* to teach us the things of God, to bring them to our remembrance, to make the things of God real in our life, to open up our understanding of these spiritual things and to the work that God has done for us. It is the Holy Spirit who makes us aware of the things that are coming to pass in the world around us and alerts us to the day and the hour in which we live. Thank God for the Holy Spirit in our lives, making God's Word come alive and making us the partakers of those rich things that God has freely given us!

7

The Work of The Holy Spirit In the World

The Holy Spirit has an important work to accomplish in the world. We have been looking at the work of the Holy Spirit in the life of the believer: conforming us into the image of Christ, opening unto us the things of God, and bringing us the agape love.

But what is the work of the Holy Spirit in the world? Jesus said in John 16:8,9: "He will reprove the world of sin, of righteousness, and of judgment." Then Jesus continues by saying, "Of sin, because they believe not on me." There is one ultimate sin that man will have to answer to God for—the sin of not believing in Jesus Christ. When Christ died, He died for the sins of the world: "All we like sheep have gone astray; we have turned every one to his own way, and the Lord has laid on Him the iniquities of us all" (Isaiah 53:6). Christ took upon Himself the sins of all mankind. He died for the sins of the world, so that there is one ultimate sin that will condemn you before God, and that is the sin of rejecting God's plan of salvation for you through Jesus Christ. Man was already condemned before Jesus came. Jesus said, "I didn't come to condemn the world; I came that the world through me might be saved. He who believes is not condemned, but he who believes not is condemned already, because *he has not believed on the only begotton Son of God."* That is the ultimate sin that will condemn a man—not believing in Jesus.

The Greatest Sin

The unpardonable sin basically boils down to this: the continual rejection of Jesus Christ as our Savior, which is actually blasphemy against the Holy Spirit because the Holy Spirit has come to reprove you of sin. He "reproves the world of sin" because it does not believe on Jesus. As He reproves us of sin, showing us that Christ is our only hope of salvation, if we continually reject the Holy Spirit's message to our heart, that is blasphemy against the Holy Spirit. If we continue in that rejection there is no forgiveness, not in this world nor in the world to come.

There is only one issue, and that is our relationship to Jesus Christ. There are some people who fancy themselves as not too bad. They are good, moral people; for the most part they are honest and have always been a faithful family person. They have never committed any great crime, and as they look at themselves they say, "I'll take my chances; I'm about as good as anybody." But in reality, if they have not received Jesus as their Savior, they are condemned; they are guilty of the worst sin—the rejection of God's plan of salvation and of His infinite love. So the Holy Spirit is in the world today to reprove the world of sin, "because," Jesus said, "they believe not on me."

Do you believe in Jesus Christ as your Savior? Have you committed your life to Him? If you believe in Him and have committed yourself to Him, you are saved. If you do not believe in Him and have not committed yourself to Him, you are condemned, and the Holy Spirit will reprove you of your sin because of your disbelief in Him.

Totally Pure

The second thing the Holy Spirit is reproving the world of is righteousness. Jesus made a very interesting statement about this. He said, "...of righteousness, because I go to my Father, and you see me no more" (John 16:10). After appearing to His disciples after His resurrection for about 40 days, Jesus led them as far as the city of Bethany and then told them that they were to go back to Jerusalem and wait there for the promise of God. They would receive power when the Holy Spirit came upon them, and they would become Christ's witnesses throughout the world. Then Jesus ascended into heaven, and a cloud received Him out of their sight. Acts 1:10,11 tells us that two men stood by them in white apparel, and they said to the disciples, "Ye men of Galilee, why stand ye gazing up into heaven? This same Jesus will come again in like manner as ye have seen Him go."

What does the ascension of Christ into heaven tell us? What was God saying to us by the ascension? God was bearing witness that this is the standard of righteousness that He will receive. Jesus lived the kind of righteous life that the Father will accept into heaven. What is it saying to you if you want to go to heaven by your own righteousnes or your own good works? The only way you will ever make it to heaven is to be as righteous, as pure, as holy as Jesus Christ. If you come anywhere beneath that standard of righteousness, you will not make it in.

When you look at it that way, you might as well give up, because even though you may be a very good person, and even though you may be the best person in your house and in your neighborhood, unless your righteousness is as perfect as that of Jesus Christ, there is no getting into heaven. That is the standard of righteousness that God will accept. The Holy Spirit is reproving the world of righteousness, Jesus said, "because I go to the Father and you see me no more."

Satan Defeated

Finally Jesus spoke of the Holy Spirit as reproving the world of judgment. The Spirit is not reproving the world of the judgment that is to come; that is not what Jesus said. He said in John 16:11, "...of judgment because the prince of this world is judged." He was not talking about the future judgment that man will have to face when death and hell deliver up the dead that are in them and they all stand before the Great White Throne judgment of God. The Holy Spirit is not talking to us about that. He is talking to us about judgment "because the prince of this world is judged." What did Jesus mean by that?

When we gave our heart to Jesus Christ and turned our life over to Him, it was not the end of our problem with sin. We still had problems because of our flesh. And Satan, knowing our weaknesses, was there to exploit these problems to their fullest. But what the Holy Spirit is testifying to us is that the prince of this world *is judged*. When Jesus went to the cross, and there bore our sins and died in our place, the prince of this world was judged, so that through our relationship to Christ we can have power over sin; it no longer needs to reign in our bodies.

Paul said that sin should no longer reign as king in our mortal bodies, but that Christ might now reign. In the second chapter of Colossians, Paul speaks of the victory of Jesus over the principalities and powers of darkness that were spoiled through the cross. He said, "having nailed the handwriting and ordinances that were against us to the cross, He spoiled the principalities and the powers [rankings of evil spirits] which are against us, having triumphed over them, making an open display of His victory in the cross."

The prince of this world was defeated at the cross. His power to control your life and to force you to do those things contrary to God's righteousness and God's way was taken away from him, so that you can enter into the victory of Jesus Christ. Now you can know freedom from sin and can have power over sin in your life. "Of judgment because the prince of this world is judged" means that the Lord has made provision for you to be free from whatever sin has been blighting your life. Paul says, "The old man [the old nature] was crucified with Christ." The prince of this world, Satan, was judged at the cross. And through our identification with Jesus Christ in our new life—through the power of His Spirit—we can be free from sin.

What If I Sin?

What does it mean if I do sin? It means that I have not taken advantage of what God has made available to me through the power of the risen Christ and the Holy Spirit. God has given to me all that is necessary to live the life that He wants me to live, but it is important that I take advantage of what God has done for me—that I exercise the power that he has given to me. This does not mean that I have sinless perfection; it does not mean that I am never going to sin again. But it means that if I do sin I cannot blame God for it and say, "Well, that's just the way God made me." All I can blame is my own failure to yield to the power of the Spirit and the victory of Christ.

I am aware that in some of your lives Satan has taken a very strong foothold. Some of you are bound by habits that have kept you in spiritual defeat all your Christian life. You have never been able to really enjoy your full joy in Christ, because there has been this sin or failure that has plagued and hounded you all the way along. I know that some of you have been praying about this for months; you have been crying out to God. You have been seeking God's help through diligent prayer, but you find that your flesh is so weak. You find yourself falling back into the old patterns, into the old path, almost to the point of despair. You are discouraged, and Satan begins to lie to you: "There's no way out. You'll never make it. You might as well give up."

You Can Conquer

But you *can* make it, for God has made victory over sin available to you through the power of the Holy Spirit. Satan was judged at the cross, so any power that Satan exercises in your life is usurped power; he has no authority or right. But he is very bold; he is very brash. He moves in where he has no right. He takes what he can, by whatever method he can, even though he has no legal right of being there because you have been purchased by Jesus Christ; you are now His possession. Satan was judged at the cross, and any power or authority that he seeks to exercise in your life is false. When you come against him in the name of Jesus Christ and in the power in the victory of Christ, Satan must yield. Because he has no legal authority or right to be there, he must submit. He has been defeated at the cross, and he must yield to the victory of Christ as you take that victory that is yours. Because Satan was judged, he has no real authority in your life at all. If you want to demand that he go, there is no way he can stay.

Let the True King Reign

God told Samuel the Prophet to go down to the house of Jesse and anoint one of Jesse's sons to be king over Israel, because God had rejected King Saul from ruling. Fearing Saul, Samuel went secretly down to the house of Jesse and had Jesse bring his sons in. The first one came in—good-looking, a big fellow—and Samuel thought to himself, "This must be the one!" But the Lord said, "No, man looks on the outward apppearance, but I look on the heart. This isn't the one." So one by one Jesse had his sons pass through, and every one the Lord rejected, until finally Samuel said, "Don't you have any more?" Jesse said, "There is just one more, but he's just a lad and he's out watching the sheep." Samuel said, "Call him."

As David came running in from following the sheep, God spoke to Samuel and said, "That's the one." David stood there as Samuel took a cruse of oil and poured it over his head; oil ran down over David as he stood there, and the anointing of God came upon him—God's anointing to reign over God's people. But it is interesting that even though God anointed David as king over Israel and the throne belonged to David, Saul was still sitting on it. For the next few years Saul did his best to drive David out, chasing David over the mountains like a partridge, until David even despaired of his own life. Saul did his best to hold on by force to that which was no longer his. But because of God's edict, Saul finally fell on his sword at Mount Gilboa, and the throne that had belonged to David for quite a while became David's, and he sat upon the throne and reigned.

God has ordained that Satan should no longer reign in your life. When you gave your life to Jesus Christ, you became His property, and God wants to reign in your life today. The prince of this world has been judged. Some of you he has been trying to hold onto for a long time; though you have submitted your life to Christ, Satan is hanging in there. It is time that you take the authority that God has given to you, and through the power of the Holy Spirit demand that Satan leave you alone. The Bible promises us that if we resist the devil, he will flee from us.

Pray Specifically

Satan not only goes in and takes what is not his, but he tries to hold onto what no longer belongs to him. He is very stubborn; he does not let go easily; so our prayers must be specific. I think that Satan really enjoys the generalized prayers of the believer. They do not even hurt. "God, save the world." That is so general that it does not get anything accomplished. You have got to be specific. "Lord, I claim the victory of Christ over this area in my life. Lord, I dedicate this area to you; I want Christ to come and sit on the throne. Thank You, Lord, for judging Satan. Thank You, Lord, for victory over him. And now, Lord, move him off; *You* move in and sit on the throne, and rule and reign in my life." Be specific.

Take and Hold!

But once Satan is driven out, he counterattacks and tries to take back the territory from which he has been driven. Jesus said that when an evil spirit goes forth from a man, he goes out through dry places seeking a house to inhabit, and, finding none, he comes back. I find that there is always that counterattack, that attempt to reestablish the foothold. So that which is *taken* in the name of Jesus Christ must be *held* in the name of Jesus Christ.

Many times a person having initial victory says,

"Oh, praise the Lord! The Lord has given me the victory!" And he lets his guard down. He thinks, "Oh, I've got it made. I don't have to worry about that anymore." Then Satan comes right back. He has been kicked out the front door, so he comes right around to the back door. He slips right in while you are in the living room shouting the victory; he comes back in through the kitchen! What we *take* we must *hold* through the power of the Holy Spirit.

8

Something More

Recently a young man came up to me and said, "I accepted Christ several years ago, but I was never too excited about it. I found reading the Bible uninteresting. In fact, my mind would wander, and I couldn't really concentrate on the Word. I never really knew what it was to worship God, and my prayer life was erratic. But since I was filled with the Spirit a few months ago, my life has completely changed. I have a great love for the things of God. I can't seem to get enough of the Word, and now I love to fellowship with the believers. What a great change has happened in my life since I was filled with the Spirit!"

This story, with variations, has been told to me hundreds of times over by those who have found that there is something more than just having the Spirit indwelling their life at conversion. We do recognize that every born-again believer has the Spirit dwelling in him. Writing in 1 Corinthians 6:19, Paul declares that our bodies are the temples of the Holy Spirit who dwells in us. He also declares in 1 Corinthians 12:3 that you cannot call Christ Lord except by the Spirit.

The Spirit and the Believer

There are three Greek prepositions used in the

New Testament to designate the different relationships of the Spirit to the believer: *para*, *en*, and *epi*. In John 14:17 Jesus said to His disciples concerning the Holy Spirit, "Ye know Him, for He dwells with [para] you and shall be in [en] you." Here a twofold relationship is expressed: *para* (with) and *en* (in). The Holy Spirit was *with* us prior to our conversion. He is the One who brought us conviction of sin and revealed Christ as the answer. When we accepted Jesus as our Savior and invited Him into our lives, the Holy Spirit began to indwell us.

But God has something more—the beautiful empowering through the *epi* relationship. Note that this is what Jesus was promising His disciples just prior to His ascension. In Luke 24:49 He said, "Behold, I send the promise of my Father upon [epi] you" or "over you." In Acts 1:8 He said, "But ye shall receive power when the Holy Spirit comes upon [epi] you."

We read in Acts 10:44 that the Holy Spirit descended "upon" the Gentile believers in the house of Cornelius: "While Peter yet spoke these words, the Holy Spirit fell upon [epi] all of them which heard the word." In Acts 19:6, when Paul laid hands upon the Ephesian believers, the Holy Spirit came upon [epi] them.

We read in Acts 8 that Philip had gone to Samaria and preached Christ unto them; many people believed Philip's preaching of the things of the kingdom of God and the name of Jesus Christ, and they were baptized. If there is just one baptism (Ephesians 4:5), then we must accept that at this point the Samaritan believers were baptized by the Spirit into the body of Christ (1 Corinthians 12:13), and the Holy Spirit began to indwell them. It is obvious, however, that there was yet a further relationship to the Holy Spirit to be received, for when the church in Jerusalem heard that the Samaritans had received the gospel, they sent Peter and John unto them that they might pray for them to receive the Holy Spirit, for as yet He had fallen upon [epi] none of them.

The Overflowing Life

When Paul came to the church in Ephesus and found that the believers' experience was lacking, possibly in love or joy and zeal, he asked them, "Did you receive the Holy Spirit when you believed?" If the full relationship with the Spirit is attained simultaneously with conversion, the question makes no sense. The question itself acknowledged a relationship deeper and beyond the conversion experience. What they were lacking was the *epi* relationship with the Holy Spirit, for that is what resulted when Paul laid his hands upon them in Acts 19:6: "and the Spirit came upon [epi] them."

Being filled with the Spirit adds new dimensions of love, joy, and exuberance to the Christian life. If Paul the Apostle would meet you and begin to share the glories of Christ with you, would he be apt to ask, "Did you receive the Spirit when you believed?" God wants your life not to just be indwelt or even filled with the Spirit. He wants your life to overflow.

The Eight-Day Feast

In John 7:37 we read, "In the last day, that great day of the feast, Jesus stood and cried, saying, 'If any man thirst, let him come unto me and drink.' " This was the Feast of the Tabernacles, the feast in which God's people remembered His divine preservation of their fathers as they wandered for 40 years in the wilderness. In Leviticus 23 we read what when they observed this feast they were to make little booths and were to move out of their houses and dwell in the booths for the eight days of the feast. As tradition developed, they were to leave enough space in the roof thatches so that they could see the stars at night, to remind them that their forefathers had slept under the stars for 40 years. Also, enough space was to be left in the walls so that the wind could blow through, so they would remember that even though their fathers were exposed to the elements for 40 years, God miraculously preserved them.

At the temple during this feast, each day the priests would make a procession to the Pool of Siloam, where they would fill their large water jugs and then come in procession up the many steps to the temple mount. As the people were singing the glorious hallel psalms, the priests would pour out the water on the pavement; this was to remind the worshipers of the water that came out of the rock in the wilderness when it was smitten by Moses, and of God's supernatural preservation of their fathers in that dry wilderness.

It is said that on the eighth day, the last day (which was known as the great day of the feast), the priests did not make a procession to the pool to fill the jugs with water. On this day there was no pouring out of water on the pavement. This also was significant, for it was an acknowledgement that God had fulfilled His promise; He had brought them into the land that was well-watered and flowing with milk and honey, and they no longer needed that miraculous supply of water out of the rock.

It was on this day, the great day of the feast, that Jesus stood and cried, saying, "If any man thirst, let him come unto me and drink!" Jesus is talking of that universal spiritual thirst that every person experiences.

Basic Human Needs

Mankind is a trinity of body, soul, and spirit. It

is difficult, if not impossible, for man to separate himself into these three entities because we are totally integrated—body, soul, and spirit—so that anything that affects me physically will affect me mentally, and can also affect me spiritually. Anything that affects me mentally also affects me physically. More and more the psychologists are discovering the close relationship between our emotions and our physical health. By the same token, whatever affects me spiritually will also affect me emotionally and physically, so that when a person is born again, it has an effect upon his whole being: spirit, soul, and body.

Abraham Maslow has identified and catalogued in order of strength our body drives, which are known as the homeostasis. These are the beautiful built-in mechanisms that God created to monitor our bodies to keep the proper balance that will sustain and perpetuate life. Maslow has identified the strongest of these drives as the air drive: the body monitors the oxygen levels in the blood and demands that oxygen be replenished when it gets too low. The body's response is to start panting as the rate of the heartbeat increases. Next in order is the thirst drive, then hunger, then bladder, then sex, and so on in a declining order. These drives all involve man's physical needs.

The sociologists have also listed what they call our sociological drives. Man thirsts, or has a drive, for love. There is also a need for security. And there is the need to be needed.

Down in the deepest part of man, in the area of his spirit, there is also a very strong thirst or drive. This is the thirst of man's spirit for a meaningful relationship with God. The attempt of the psychologist to understand human behavior will always be limited until he recognizes the spiritual dimension of man. The strongest drive and the deepest need of man is to know God. In Psalm 42:1,2 David said, "As the heart panteth after the water brooks, so panteth my soul after Thee, O God. My soul thirsteth for God, for the living God." Paul declared in Philippians 3:7,8 that everything that was once important to him he counted loss for the excellency of the knowledge of Jesus Christ. Paul explains in Romans 8 how God has made man subject to emptiness; he was deliberately designed that way so that man could never be complete apart from God. Nature seeks to fill the vacuum, so man by nature has sought to fill this spiritual void with a variety of physical or emotional experiences.

The Needs Are Distinct

The thirsts we experience are separate and distinct, so that we cannot satisfy a physical thirst with an emotional experience. If you were lost in the desert, walking across the hot sand, and the moisture level of your body was getting dangerously low, you would feel a tremendous physical thirst. As your body dehydrated, you would lose your strength. Let us say that you are finally lying in the hot sand, instinctively digging for water, when someone comes over the sand dune, spies you there, and says, "Oh, I know who you are. I want you to know that I have had a secret love for you. I think you are the greatest person in the world, and I love you tremendously."

While this person might be fulfilling your emotional need for love, you are dying of thirst in his arms, for you cannot satisfy a physical thirst with an emotional experience. In the same way, you cannot satisfy an emotional thirst with a physical experience, and this has created some problems in our present society.

One-Sided Fulfillment

We are living in a culture in which most of the physical needs of the person are being adequately cared for; yet quite often there is a tragic lack of fulfillment of the emotional needs. Many times parents have difficulty understanding their children's actions of rebellion against the home. I have heard them say, "I've given my child everything; I cannot understand how he can do what he is doing." When they declare, "I've given him everything," they are usually talking about physical things: the child has received several bicycles and his own television set, stereo, and car.

But so often these things were given to the child in order to push him away. The purpose was to keep the child entertained by these things so that parental time would not have to be given him—time which would cause him to feel the closeness of love within the family. The mother so often says, "Why don't you go into your room and watch television? Don't you know you're making me nervous? Don't ask so many questions. Why don't you go outside and ride your bicycle?" The child, thirsting for love and security, is pushed away to the material things, and one day he ultimately rebels against the material world, as we saw in the counterculture revolution known as the hippie movement.

You cannot satisfy an emotional thirst with a physical experience. It is also true that, down deep, man has a deep spiritual thirst for God. One of the problems of our present age is that man has endeavored to satisfy that deep thirst for God with physical or emotional experiences. This deep thirst for God is one of the reasons behind the pleasure mania in the world today. People are trying to satisfy that deep need for God with emotional and physical experiences. It also partially explains drug abuse, as people often have pseudospiritual experiences through the use of drugs. Many of the people using LSD thought they were having true experiences with God.

The Deep Universal Thirst

When Jesus said, "If any man thirst," He was referring to that deep universal thirst of man's spirit for God. It is interesting to me that some psychology textbooks identify frustration as one of the root causes of neurotic behavior. They declare that a person's problem often begins with frustration, that feeling that you have not attained what life is all about, that there must be more to life than what you have experienced—but what is it and how do I attain it? It is reaching out for something I am not sure of, and not finding what I am hoping for. What is frustration but thirst, spiritual thirst, that deep thirst in man's spirit for God?

The psychology books show how frustration leads to an inferiority complex, which is nothing more than my rationale to myself as to why I have not achieved this satisfaction or fulfillment that I long for. I say, "If only I had money," or "If only I had blue eyes instead of brown," or "If only I had attained a better education." With these or a thousand other excuses I explain to myself the reason for my frustration.

Two Kinds of Escapes

According to the textbooks, I then move from my inferiority complex to an escape. This can be overt or invert. The inverted escapes are manifested in attempts to build a wall around your true self. You will often display to other people a facade which is far different from the real you. You act as if it does not hurt when it really does; you act very confident when in reality you are scared. You begin to keep people at a distance; you are afraid they might find the true you. You avoid the person whom you feel is moving in too close to you. You do not want to speak to him when he calls. You get to the point where you do not want to answer the doorbell. In its final form the invert escape is manifested in the hermit living alone in his shack in the desert, firing shotgun blasts at anyone who comes beyond his gate with the "Keep Out—No Trespassing" signs.

The overt escapes are manifested in many forms, such as alcoholism, drug abuse, compulsive eating or gambling, nomadism, extramarital affairs, etc. I cannot bear to face the reality of my failure to find true fulfillment, so I escape into unreality. These escapes then bring me to a guilt complex. I know that what I am doing is wrong. I know it is destroying me and those around me who love me, yet I do not seem to have the capacity to stop. I begin to hate myself for what I am doing to myself and others.

The guilt complex then moves into a subconscious desire for punishment. This is usually manifested in a neurotic behavior pattern designed to bring the disapproval of my associates, which I interpret as punishment, which in turn relieves me from my feelings of guilt. When I was a child, my father took care of my guilt complex by punishing me. In my case it usually took the form of a spanking. Once I had been punished I no longer felt guilty and I could take my place as a member in good standing in the family. Prior to the punishment, I felt a strained relationship and a sense of alienation.

As we grow older there is no parental authority over us, so to be relieved of guilt we must behave in an unacceptable way to bring rebuke or rejection, which we interpret as punishment. Once punished, we feel free from our guilt complex and then return to our frustration and begin the cycle over again. When Jesus said, "If any man thirst," He was referring to this thirst in man's spirit for God, that which the psychologists classify as frustration.

True Quenching of Thirst

When Jesus was talking to the woman of Samaria, He asked her for a drink, and she challenged Him for asking, since He was a Jew and she was a Samaritan. By tradition they were not to have any dealings with each other. Jesus responded to her, "If you knew who it was that was asking you for a drink, you would have asked Him for a drink." She answered rather smartly, "Why would I ask you for a drink when you have nothing to draw with, and this well is very deep?" Jesus then said to her, "He who drinks of this water will thirst again." I believe that this verse should be inscribed over every goal, ambition, or pursuit of pleasure that a man has. You may drink of that water, achieve your goal, realize your ambition, and fulfill your fantasies, but you are going to thirst again. It will not satisfy, for way down deep your spirit is thirsting after God, and nothing can satisfy that thirst except a meaningful relationship with God.

When Jesus said, "If any man thirst, let him come unto me and drink," He was expressing the gospel in its simplest terms. He was saying to all of mankind, "Deep down within your life you need God. You are reaching out for a meaningful relationship with God. Come unto me, and your thirst will not only be fully satisfied and fulfilled, but out of your life there will gush torrents of living water." Only Christ can satisfy your spiritual thirst, for He brings you into a meaningful relationship with God.

Torrents of Water

In John 7:38 Jesus went on to say, "He that believeth on me, as the Scripture hath said, out of his belly shall flow rivers of living water." The Greek words here are a little more intense than what is reflected in the King James Version. The Lord is literally declaring that, if a person believes on Him, "Out of his belly there will gush torrents of living water"—not just a gentle little stream flowing out, but a tremendous torrent of water, as that which cascades down a mountain ravine during a cloudburst.

To what was Jesus making reference when He spoke of "torrents of living water" coming forth from our life? When John wrote this Gospel, it was several years after the fact. His was one of the last New Testament books to be written, and John was writing with the advantage of hindsight. At the actual time Jesus was talking about the torrents of living water, John was probably confused as to what Jesus meant or what He was promising the people. But because John wrote the Gospel with understanding gained through the advantage of hindsight, he added his own commentary expressed in the brackets of verse 39, in which he explained that Jesus was speaking of the Holy Spirit, "which they that believe on Him should receive; for the Holy Spirit was not yet given, because Jesus was not yet glorified." So Jesus was talking about the empowering of the believer's life by the Holy Spirit.

God's Desire for You

I think we have to accept without question the fact that this description is much more than just the indwelling presence of the Spirit within a believer's life at conversion. It is one thing to have the Holy Spirit indwelling your life; it is another thing to have that glorious, dynamic power of God's Spirit flowing forth from your life like a torrent of living water.

God has a fuller relationship for you than just the indwelling of the Spirit. It is God's desire that the Spirit flow forth from your life. It really makes little difference what you term it. Some call it the baptism of the Holy Spirit, some call it the filling of the Holy Spirit, and some call it the empowering by the Holy Spirit. It really does not matter what you call it; what is important is that you have that glorious outpouring of the power of the Spirit flowing forth from your life.

God always looks at man in two ways. First, God looks at him *subjectively,* as He seeks to do His work in your life. But God's purposes are never culminated in His subjective work. God also looks toward that *objective* work which He seeks to do through you. He works in you *subjectively* that He might work through you *objectively.* He desires to do a work *in* you and *for* you in order that He might work *through* you to touch others. Our relationship to the Spirit is never complete when He is just indwelling us. We are more than vessels to contain the Spirit of God. God desires that we might be *channels* through which His Spirit might flow.

The Power in Action

As you look at your own experience and relationship to the Holy Spirit, if you cannot say that the powerful dynamic of God's Spirit is gushing forth from your life like a river or torrents of living water, then God has a fuller relationship to His Spirit that He desires to bring into your life, and I would encourage you to seek this power of God's Spirit until it flows forth from your life. There is a needy world around us which needs to be touched by the power of God's Spirit flowing forth from us. If you object to calling it the baptism of the Holy Spirit, call it whatever you like, but what Jesus is describing is far more than the mere indwelling of the Holy Spirit in the life of the believer experienced at the time of his conversion. That beautiful flowing of the Spirit from a person's life is the true *charisma.*

9

Speaking in Tongues

One of the areas of sharpest controversy within the body of Christ today involves speaking with other tongues, "glossalalia." At one extreme are people who label any exercise of tongues as satanic. At the other extreme are people who declare that you are not filled or baptized with the Holy Spirit unless you speak with other tongues. They declare that speaking in tongues is the initial evidence of the baptism of the Holy Spirit. In 1 Corinthians 13:1 Paul declares that tongues in themselves are not a valid evidence of the Holy Spirit within the life of a believer, for, "Though I speak with the tongues of men and of angels, and have not love [agape], I am become as sounding brass or a clanging cymbal." In other words, the tongues are only meaningless sounds and have no validity if there is not that accompanying agape love.

Tongues Versus No Tongues

In the book of Acts, speaking in tongues often accompanied the *epi* relationship to the Holy Spirit. Such is the case in Acts chapters 2, 10, and 19. However, in the eighth chapter of Acts, when the Samaritan believers received the Holy Spirit, there is no mention that they spoke in tongues. However, it is obvious that there must have been some kind of phenomena that accompanied their receiving the Holy Spirit, for Simon the sorcerer was seeking to buy the power that Peter and John possessed; he desired that he might also be able to lay hands upon people that they might receive the Holy Spirit. It is evident that some kind of phenomena accompanied their receiving the Spirit because Simon wanted to buy the power so he could duplicate the feat.

Later, in Acts 9:17, when Ananais laid his hands upon Saul (Paul) that he might receive the gift of the Holy Spirit, there is no mention of Paul speaking in tongues. However, we do know that subsequently, as Paul was writing to the Corinthians, he thanked God that he spoke in tongues more than all of the Corinthians. When Paul first experienced the gift of tongues is not divulged.

We must point out that a person who speaks in tongues and lacks agape love has less valid evidence of the indwelling or the filling of the Spirit in his life than a person who has never spoken in tongues and yet manifests love and other dynamic qualities of God's Spirit. I cannot deny the validity of the Spirit-filled lives of many of those dynamic leaders and laymen in the church today who have never enjoyed the experience of speaking in tongues, and I prefer their fellowship over many who promote the speaking in tongues as the only true evidence of the Spirit-filled life, but whose personal lives are marred by strife or pride and often even heresy.

When Paul wrote to the Galatians he declared, "The fruit of the Spirit is love." The real proof of God's Spirit filling a person's life is love. Love is the most valid evidence that a man is truly filled with the Spirit, and tongues without love are just meaningless sounds.

Building, Praising, Praying

Speaking in tongues is a very edifying experience

to the believer. Paul tells us in 1 Corinthians 14:4, "He who speaks in an unknown tongue edifies himself." The term "edify" means to build up, and it is used in the New Testament for the building up of Christ within the life of the church or of the believer. The purpose of the church assembling together is to be built up in Christ, and when I am in church I should seek to build up the whole body of Christ. Personal devotions are intended to build up myself in Christ; when I speak in tongues in my personal devotions it is one of the ways by which Christ is built up within me.

Speaking in tongues is also an excellent way to praise the Lord. I often find that I have difficulty in expressing to God the feelings I have within. God has been so good, and has blessed me so much, that to merely say, "Oh God, I thank You for all that You have done," falls so far short of my feeling of deep gratitude and praise. I find difficulty in expressing these deepest feelings of my spirit. It is wonderful to be able by the Spirit to express my praises to God without having to limit it to the narrowed channel of my own intellect. Paul tells us that, when we speak in tongues, we are blessing God with the Spirit. However, if we do it in church without an interpreter, the person who is occupying the position of the unlearned cannot say "Amen" at my giving of thanks, as he does not understand what I am saying. Paul points out, "You indeed give thanks well." In other words, Paul is declaring that it is a good way to give thanks to God and to express your worship and praise to Him.

As Paul writes to the Ephesians about the Christian's spiritual warfare, he tells of the armor that we are to put on. Then he goes on to tell how we are to wage warfare against the enemy: "Praying always with all prayer and supplication in the Spirit"

(Ephesians 6:18). In verses 20 and 21 of his epistle, Jude exhorts us to keep ourselves in the love of God. He tells us that one of the ways by which we keep ourselves in His love is by praying in the Holy Spirit. In Romans 8:26 Paul tells us that one of the weaknesses that we experience in our Christian walk comes in our prayer life, by not always knowing how we ought to pray in a given situation. Many times we do not know God's will. I want to pray according to God's will because I know that prayer apart from God's will has no value. We do know that if we ask anything according to His will, He hears us. But that is where the problem arises, and that is our weakness: we do not always know what the will of God is.

Paul tells us in Romans 8 that the Holy Spirit helps these infirmities when we do not know how we ought to pray, for the Spirit Himself will make intercession for us with groanings which cannot be uttered. He is searching the heart and He knows what is the mind of the spirit, because He makes intercession for the saints according to the will of God.

So when I do not know how to pray for a particular problem, I can just groan in my spirit, and though I do not understand the groanings, yet God interprets them Himself as intercession and prayer according to His will for that person or particular situation over which I am groaning. Now if God understands the inarticulate groanings of the spirit as intercession and prayer according to His will, surely those articulated words in another tongue, though an unknown tongue to me, are nevertheless understandable by God.

Tongues in Private

We cannot challenge the statement of Paul that he

thanked God that he spoke in tongues more than all of the Corinthian believers. Yet Paul declared that, when he was in church, he would rather speak five words in a known tongue than 10,000 words in an unknown tongue. There are those who declare that, since the gifts of the Spirit were given to benefit the whole body, as Paul declares in 1 Corinthians 12:7, any private use of any of the gifts of the Spirit is forbidden and is wrong. Since Paul exercised the gift of tongues more than all the Corinthians (14:18) yet refused to exercise the gift in church (14:19), it must be assumed that he prayed and sang with the Spirit in his own private devotions.

Since the gift of speaking in tongues builds up the believer who is exercising the gift, and it is preferable that he not exercise the gift in a public assembly and is even forbidden to do so if there is no interpreter, the only place left for the exercise of this gift is in his own personal devotions. Paul said, "Speak unto yourself and unto God," so that it is proper to exercise this gift for one's own edification, as Paul did.

As you are built up in Christ, you will become an instrument through which the whole body may be edified. For when one member of the body is honored, all the members rejoice with it.

The Abuse of Tongues

Some people say they have no control over their outbursts in tongues, and so many times they just start speaking in tongues in a public service, interrupting the sermon. Sometimes these erratic outbursts come in conversations with friends. I had a lady tell me that when she received the gift of tongues, she had no control over it. The next day, when the gas man came to read her meter, she went out to talk to him about a problem with the service.

Then she started speaking to him in tongues. He looked at her rather weirdly, and finally turned and hurried out of the yard. She told me she could not control her speaking in tongues.

Scripture tells us in 1 Corinthians 14:32 that the spirits of the prophets are subject to the prophets. I believe this is declaring that we are always in control of ourselves when exercising any of the gifts of the Spirit. Paul instructs us in 1 Corinthians 14:28 that if there is no interpreter present, the person should keep silent in the church, and speak to himself and to God. Paul is calling for control over the gift; he is saying that a person does not have to speak out, that it is possible for him to just speak to himself and to God. In verse 15 Paul also declared that he would pray with the Spirit, and he would pray with understanding also, showing that the speaking in tongues was actually controlled by the exercise of his own will. When he willed, he could speak in tongues; when he willed, he could speak in one of the languages that he understood and knew.

In some church services the sermon is interrupted by an utterance in tongues. But there is no Scriptural basis at all for these types of interruptions. In fact, Paul said, "Let all things be done decently and in order." I cannot see that these kinds of interruptions are ever in order. They are, on the other hand, very rude and extremely distracting. There is really no need for the Holy Spirit to bring forth an utterance in tongues during the ministry of the Word of God, for the minister himself should be speaking by the anointing of the Holy Spirit and exercising, as it were, the gift of prophecy as he is speaking forth God's truth to the people. When a person stands up and interrupts God's messenger, he is putting the Holy Spirit in the awkward position of interrupting Himself to interject another thought or idea. Such unscriptural uses of the gift of tongues is another form of *charismania*.

Tongues and Interpretations

Unquestionably, Paul is seeking to restrict the use of the gift of tongues in the church. There has developed what I feel to be a false concept of "messages" in tongues, as though God has a special message for the church to be given through tongues and interpretation. This is how they are usually referred to when they are given in church—as a message in tongues. There is not one single instance in the New Testament that we can point to as an example of where God spoke to anyone through tongues and interpretations, or just through tongues themselves.

Most often, when there is a public utterance of tongues which is to be followed by an interpretation, rarely is a true interpretation of the tongues given.

I grew up in a Pentecostal church, and I am convinced that during all of my years in the church, I rarely heard a true interpretation of the multitudes of utterances in tongues. If I ever did in those early years, I am not aware of it. There were long utterances in tongues followed by short interpretations. There were short utterances in tongues followed by long interpretations. It was always explained to me that there is a difference between interpreting and translation, which I readily accept. However, I would note that, in the utterance in tongues, oftentimes it would be just one phrase repeated over and over again. Yet the supposed interpretation would have no repetition of a phrase.

To Whom Are Tongues Addressed?

In 1 Corinthians 14:2 Paul tells us that he who

speaks in an unknown tongue "does not speak to men, but unto God, for no man understands him; howbeit, in the Spirit he is speaking mysteries [or divine secrets]." Here he points out that tongues are definitely addressed to God. In all cases of the use of tongues in the New Testament, we find that they were addressed to God. On the Day of Pentecost in Acts 2:11, those who could understand the languages were remarking that these people were declaring the wonderful works of God. They were not using tongues to preach, but were using them to glorify God as they were declaring His glorious works. In 1 Corinthians 14:14 Paul declares that tongues are used in his prayers to God. In 14:16 he declares that they are used to bless God, and finally, to give thanks unto God.

But there is not a single reference where the gift was used to address man by either preaching or teaching; we find that they were always addressed to God, it would of necessity follow that a true interpretation would also be addressed to God. The interpretation would be of the prayer, thanksgiving, praise, or declaring of the glory of God. It would often sound as one of David's Psalms declaring God's glory. Paul said, "If you give an utterance in tongues and there is no interpreter, how is the person sitting in the seat of the unlearned going to say yes and amen at your giving of thanks, seeing he does not understand what you say?"

Notice that Paul declares that you are giving thanks to God, not giving a message to the church; but I cannot even say amen to your giving of thanks if I do not understand what you are saying. Thus there is the necessity of the interpretation if there is a public utterance of tongues, so that the whole body might be edified.

Tongues Versus Prophecy

In contrast to this, Paul tells us that he who prophesies is speaking to men for edification, exhortation, and comfort (1 Corinthians 14:3). As I have studied this definition of prophecy, I have concluded that most of the so-called interpretations that we hear in the Pentecostal or charismatic services are actually the exercise of the gift of prophecy, because they so often run along the line, "Thus saith the Lord, 'My little children, call upon my name' or 'Praise me.' " They are exhorting the people to praise, give thanks, worship, or they are comforting the people in the goodness and grace of God. When the words are addressed to the church to edify, or comfort, this falls in the category of prophecy rather than interpretation of tongues.

I have concluded that when a person gives an utterance in tongues, rather than praying that there might be an interpretation, so often the prayer is, "O God, speak to us." If God speaks to us through a gift of the Spirit, it is usually through the gift of prophecy, word of wisdom, or knowledge. We find so often that the utterance in tongues gives faith to the person with the gift of prophecy, and he stands up and exercises his gift of prophecy rather than giving an interpretation of what was said in the tongues.

Paul declares that, if everyone is speaking in tongues in church and a stranger would come in, he would say that everybody is crazy. Paul also restricts the use of tongues in church to two or at the most three utterances, and those in turn. If there is no one with the gift of interpretation present, Paul completely forbids the public use of tongues, telling the person that he should keep silent and speak to himself and God, which also implies a person's control over the exercise of the gift.

One Result of Tongues

Several years ago, when Calvary Chapel of Costa Mesa was quite small, we were meeting on Sunday nights in a clubhouse. On a particular Sunday evening (which was Pentecost Sunday), at the close of the lesson as we were softly worshiping God together, I asked one of the ladies in the fellowship if she would worship God in the Spirit, since I knew that when she spoke in tongues she usually spoke in French. As she began to worship God, I could understand enough of her French to know that she was thanking God for her new life in Christ and the beautiful new song of love He had given her. I thought this was especially beautiful, as she used to be a nightclub singer prior to her conversion. At the conclusion of her worship in the Spirit, my wife began to give the interpretation to the group, and knowing that she does not know French, I was particularly blessed to hear how accurately the worship with the Spirit was being interpreted for the fellowship.

After the meeting one of the young men in the fellowship brought a Jewish girl from Palm Springs for counseling. When we sat down together, she said, "Before we get to my problems, explain to me what was happening here tonight. Why did the one lady speak to God in French, and the other lady translate to the group what she said?" I said, "Would you believe that neither of those ladies knows French?" I told her that I knew for a fact that neither knew French, since one of them was a close friend and the other was my wife. I then showed her in 1 Corinthians where it speaks of the gift of tongues and interpretation. She then told me that she had lived in France for six years, and that the French spoken was in the perfect accent of what she called the Aristocratic French. She also stated that the translation was perfect. She then said, "I must accept Jesus Christ now, before we go any further."

It was my joy to see her find her Messiah and become a member of the body of Christ. There was a demonstration of the gift of tongues, followed by the true interpretation, which was glorious praise and worship of God. The result was the edifying of the body and in this case the conversion of this Jewish girl.

10

When Are Tongues to Cease?

Those religious doctrines which forbid speaking with tongues usually point to 1 Corinthians 13:8, where we are told, "Whether there be tongues, they shall cease," as the basis for their prohibition. When tongues would cease, however, is dependent on how the phrase "that which is perfect is come" is interpreted. Those who use this verse to prohibit tongues interpret "that which is perfect" as the full revelation of the Canon of Scripture, concluding with the Revelation of Jesus Christ given to John. Their argument usually assumes that, until the Canon of Scripture was complete, these gifts were used to instruct the early church. But once Scripture was complete, they no longer needed to depend on these gifts. Thus tongues ceased when Scripture was completed.

Answers to the Argument

This argument at first sounds plausible; however, it is nothing more than hypothetical speculation, and it is not only void of Scriptural foundation but it would appear to be against all Scriptural use of the gift in the New Testament. Not once do we find speaking in tongues used to instruct believers in the New Testament. On the contrary, we read in 1 Corinthians 14:2 that those who spoke in tongues were not speaking to man but to God. They also were not to speak in tongues in the church unless someone with the gift of interpretation were present, so that everyone present might be able to say yes and amen to the blessing and giving of thanks offered to God.

The use of the gift of tongues in Scripture has never had any association with teaching God's truth to the church. There could therefore be no relationship between the gift of tongues ceasing and the arrival of the full Canon of Scripture. One of the cardinal rules of Scripture interpretation is to examine the text in light of its context. To know the text, read the context. The context of 1 Corinthians 13 is the supremacy of love. It is supreme over the exercise of the gifts of the Spirit, which are void without love (verses 1-3). Love is next defined in verses 4-7, and then the never-failing quality of love is declared in verses 8-12, showing that it will outlast tongues, prophecies, and knowledge. Finally, in verse 13 the abiding trilogy of faith, hope, and love is presented, claiming love as supreme.

The immedite context is the unfailing nature of love in contrast to prophecies (which would fail), and tongues (which would cease), and knowledge (which would vanish away). Prophecies and knowledge are partial, but when that which is perfect is come, we will no longer have obscured vision, but will see face to face. Our knowledge will no longer be partial knowledge, but complete, because we then will know even as we are known.

The idea that the Greek word *teleios*, translated "perfect," referred to the full Canon of Scipture did not occur to some of the greatest of all Greek scholars from the past century. It is more of an invention or creation of recent vintage to counteract the modern tongues movement. Thayer, in his *Greek-English Lexicon*, says of *teleios* as used in 1 Corinthians 13:10, "The perfect state of all things to be ushered in by the return of Christ from heaven." Alford, in his *New Testament for English Readers,* says of it, "At the Lord's coming and after." When the only Scriptural basis for rejecting the validity of speaking in tongues rests on such a questionable and tenuous interpretation of the Greek word *teleios,* which was wrested from the context in which it is used, one has to sincerely challenge the expositional honesty of such scholarship. To be kind, I will say that at best it is prejudicial blindness—not at all scholarly or conclusive.

It should also be noted that, simultaneously with the tongues ceasing in 1 Corinthians 13:8, it declared that prophecies would fail and knowledge would vanish away. Is anyone willing to admit that God no longer speaks to the church to edify, exhort, or comfort it? Has knowledge vanished away? The Scriptures declare that we know in part. Some seem to pretend to perfect knowledge, but I seriously doubt their pretensions. We will not know even as we are known until Christ comes again.

The Spirit in Church History

Since there is no solid Scriptural basis for denying the validity of speaking in tongues today, what other basis do we have to challenge the exercise of this gift? There is always the alleged absence of its use in the subsequent history of the church. This is not true, however, for throughout the history of the church the issue seemed to crop up every now and then. There are reports of speaking in tongues among zealous groups throughout church history. Its seeming absence of practice during much of church history is not a strong witness against its validity. I personally am not proud of the traditional church history. It seems to me that it is the story of failure. The New Testament church thrived during the apostolic age; Paul was able to report to the Colossians that the truth of the gospel had gone into all the world and was bearing fruit (Colossians 1:6). With the guidance and empowering of the Spirit they were able to take the gospel to all the world in the first century. This is a feat which the traditional church has not been able to duplicate in all the subsequent ages.

It is tragic that many people seek to relegate the special power of the Holy Spirit to the apostolic period only, and have now substituted the genius and programs of man to accomplish Christ's Great Commission. The result has been the dismal failure of the church. One must seriously question if it was God's plan or man's pride to set aside the dependency upon the guidance and the power of the Holy Spirit to reach the lost world for Jesus Christ.

Paul said to the Galatians, "Are you so foolish? Having begun in the Spirit, are you now made perfect by the flesh?" (Galatians 3:3). This is precisely what is being declared by those who would relegate the operations of the gifts of the Spirit to the apostolic age only. The church, they say, was begun in the Spirit to help them overcome all the obstacles of the pagan, hostile world. But once seminaries and organizational structures were established, they no longer needed that power of the Spirit. The church could now be perfected by the trained men. An honest look at church history should dispel that fallacy once and for all.

Joel's Promise

As we consider the promise of the Spirit in Joel 2:28, and as we read the whole context of that promise, we see that he was referring to the last days. The prophecy actually carries right into the tribulation period, with the sun turning to darkness and the moon to blood, and onto the coming great day of the Lord, when that which is perfect has come. What began at Pentecost was obviously to continue to the coming again of Jesus Christ. Peter confirmed this when he spoke to the inquiring throng on the Day of Pentecost who were asking, "What shall we do?" He commanded, "Repent and be baptized, every one of you, in the name of Jesus Christ for the remission of sins, and you shall receive the gift of the Holy Spirit. For the promise [the promise in Joel] is unto you and to your children, and to all who are afar off, as many as the Lord our God shall call" (Acts 2:38,39). Nothing was said about a cutoff date at the end of the apostolic period. That idea is an invention of man to excuse the lack of power in their churches and in their lives today.

We certainly are not advocating that everyone speak in tongues. Paul, through his rhetorical question, "Do all speak in tongues?" (1 Corinthiians 12:30), expected a "no" answer, even as all do not have the gifts of healing. On the other hand, I feel that it is wrong to forbid, or even discourage, the speaking in tongues by those who want to use the gift to assist them in their prayer life or personal devotions to God.

11

Why Charisma Often Becomes Charismania

In Ephesians 4 Paul tells us that God has placed in the church certain gifted men, such as pastor-teachers, to perfect the saints for the work of the ministry and to build up the body of Christ. The end result of sound teaching is to bring the believers into a fully matured state so they will not be carried about with every wind of doctrine.

One of the greatest weaknesses of the charismatic movement is its lack of sound Bible teaching. There seems to be an undue preoccupation with experience, which is often placed above the Word. As a consequence, charismatics have become a fertile field for strange and unscriptural doctrines proliferating through their ranks.

It is of utmost importance that we allow the Bible to be the final authority for our faith and practice. Any time we begin to allow experiences to become the criteria for doctrine or belief, we have lost Biblical authority, and the inevitable result is confusion. There are so many people today who witness of remarkable and exciting experiences. The Mormons, for example, "bear witness" to the experience of the truth of the Book of Mormon. They encourage people to pray in order to experience whether or not their Book of Mormon is true. One person says he has experienced that it is true, and another says he has experienced that it is false. Which one am I to believe? Each swears he has had a true experience from God; yet one has to be wrong. Whenever you open the door for experience to become the foundation or criterion for doctrinal truth, you are opening a Pandora's box. The result is that the truth is lost in the conflicting experiences, and the inevitable consequence is total confusion. We know that God is not the Author of confusion.

Slain in the Spirit?

One of the experiences that is quite common among charismatics is the practice of being "slain in the Spirit." I have never discovered the supposed value of this experience. Yet it is quite a common occurrence among charismatics. When pressed for a Scriptural basis, they usually mention the soldiers who came to arrest Jesus in the garden. When Jesus asked them, "Who are you looking for?" they responded, "Jesus of Nazareth." He answered them, "I am He," and they fell backward to the ground. But note that they were unbelievers, not Spirit-filled members of the body of Christ. (There is no indication that they ever became believers.) This is certainly not a Scriptural basis for the practice among believers today.

Often charismatics refer to the Apostle Paul on the road to Damascus. Again, Paul at that time was an enemy of Christ. There was no evangelist or pastor laying hands on him, nor do we ever read of the experience being repeated after his conversion. Paul also had a vital personal encounter with Jesus Christ as the Lord spoke to him audibly during his experience.

When I was young I attended many services

where people were supposedly being slain in the Spirit. I often had hands laid on me; quite often there was a gentle pressure exerted on the forehead, pushing me backward. With some of the evangelists, it was not quite so gentle. If you stand with your eyes closed, hands lifted, and your head tilted back, it does not take much pressure for you to go over backward, especially if you know that someone is standing behind to catch you!

Exorcising Demons?

Another popular pastime among many charismatic groups is the discerning and exorcising of demons out of each other. Numerous books and articles have been written on this subject by their recognized leaders, and a whole doctrine developed upon the basis of experiences alone. One of the evangelists who was thought to be especially gifted in this ministry reportedly began to pass out Kleenex tissues in his services so that the people might regurgitate the demons into the Kleenex! If in a meeting one of the group began to yawn, this was a sign that he was possessed by a demon of lethargy. To burp would invite the exorcism of the demon of gluttony, which would invade you the moment you ate one bite more food than you needed. Much damage has been done to sensitive people through this pernicious doctrine, and scattered across the world today are many tragic victims of its aftermath.

In one of the books I read on this subject, the author spoke of how we were to consign these demons to the pit when we cast them out. And how did he know we had the power to send them to the pit? While he was in conversation with a demon, prior to casting it out, the demon begged him not to send it to the pit. He then asked the demon if he had the authority, and the demon answered yes. He thus declared on the authority of what the demon told him that he could command all demons to go to the pit. If Satan is the father of all lies, how could you trust the word of one of his emissaries to be true? Here a doctrine was being based upon the supposed word of a demon.

Bible Doctrine Versus Demon Doctrine

Paul warned against doctrines of demons in the last days. This whole doctrine and practice was developed entirely upon experiences, with no solid Scriptural foundation. Many people have testified to me of the great victory they experienced after having been delivered from some demon. Should we then believe that we can have victory over our flesh life by having the demon of lust cast out? Does the Bible teach that I as a child of God can be possessed by a demon, and are there instances in the New Testament where in the church gatherings they cast demons out of each other? To the contrary, there are passages that indicate that a child of God *cannot* be possessed by demons.

Paul, writing to the Corinthians, said that our bodies are the temples of the Holy Spirit which is in us (1 Corinthians 6:19). He also asked what communion light has with darkness, and what concord Christ has with Belial, and what agreement the temple of God has with idols (2 Corinthians 6:14-16). In 1 Corinthians 10:20 he identifies idols with demons, and in verse 21 he declares, "You cannot drink the cup of the Lord and the cup of devils." When faced with these Scriptures, many charismatics who were following these practices developed the doctrine that the demons could invade the believer's mind but not his spirit. This concept is also without Scriptural basis. There is no account in the Scriptures of a born-again believer in Jesus Christ being exorcised of a demon.

That demons can and do possess the bodies of *unbelievers* is an accepted fact of Scripture, and that they can be exorcised through the authority of the name of Jesus is also evident. But to believe that a child of God can be freed from the problems of the flesh (such as lust, anger, and envy) by exorcism is charismania.

Written Versus Spoken

Many charismatics seem to prefer the spoken word over the written Word, and they seek to show the power of the *rhema* over the *logos.* The ministry of the prophet or exhorter is preferred above that of the teacher. The anointing of the Spirit is preferred above that of the teacher. The anointing of the Spirit is recognized not so much by the truth that is unfolded as by the fervency and excitement displayed by the speaker. If the voice is loud and pitched high, and the speech very forceful and rapid, this is the sign of the true anointing, especially if he sucks a lot of air between phrases and throws in amens and hallelujahs between thoughts! Some of the more adept evangelists have developed great skills in whipping the people into a high state of excitement bordering upon hysteria by just repeating a single phrase, such as "Praise the Lord," using different voice intonations.

Because of the preference for the spoken word, tongues with interpretation or a prophetic utterance is desired above the preaching or teaching of the Scriptures. In many charismatic fellowships, if there have not been manifestations of these vocal gifts, the people do not recognize or acknowledge the moving of the Spirit in that service. I have often heard people say that the Spirit moved in such a powerful way in the service that the preacher did not even have an opportunity to speak. This idea is used to express the "ultimate" in the moving of God's Spirit.

Spiritual Versus Soulish

Much of man's worship experience is more soulish than spiritual. Within typical church liturgy there is much that appeals to the soulish nature of man. The ornate robes, the choral chants, the candles and incense—all move me to a pleasant psychic experience of reverence. On the other end of the spectrum, the uncontrolled release of the emotions, with shouting, clapping, and dancing, moves other people to strong psychic experiences. It is possible that neither truly touches my spirit. In Hebrews 4:12 we read that the Word of God is sharper than a two-edged sword, and is able to divide between the soul and the spirit. It is God's Word that ministers to the spirit of man and feeds the spirit. So if the minister is not given the opportunity to share God's Word, we must legitimately question if the soul of man or the Spirit of God was moving in the service.

It is sad that unscriptural excesses are so freely tolerated among charismatics. Often, hungry and sincere believers who sense a lack of power in their lives will go to their services with an open, hungry heart seeking God's power, but when they observe the absence of solid Scriptural content and the presence of distasteful fleshly manifestations, they turn their backs on the whole valid and beautiful work of God's Spirit that a person can experience in his life.

Exalting the Flesh

I know that in my flesh dwells no good thing. One of the greatest problems in my spiritual walk is my flesh. My flesh wants to be recognized and admired.

The flesh will even seek glory and attention in a spiritual atmosphere. My flesh wants people to think that I am more spiritual than I really am, that I pray more than I really do. It makes me feel good when someone says, "You know the Word so well; have you memorized the whole Bible?" I like to hear them say, "You are such a great man of prayer," even though I know I am not.

Jesus warned us in Matthew 6 to take heed that we do not perform our righteous acts before man to be seen of man. This "to be seen of man" is a strong motivating force, and I must continually guard against it. Jesus then mentioned that the desire to be seen of man is behind much of our giving, praying, and spiritual activities, such as fasting. We are told in the Scriptures that one day all our works are to be tested by fire to be determined of what sort they are, or the motives behind them. It is very wise for us to examine our motives, for if we will judge ourselves, we will not be judged by God.

Many of the things done in charismatic services are done to draw attention to the individual. The person who shouts "Hallelujah!" and thrusts his hand upward is drawing attention to himself, and many times distracts those who are truly worshiping God. As the group sings choruses of praise, often one or more persons will stand with eyes closed and hands upraised while the others are still seated. This looks very spiritual, as does praying on a street corner, but it is drawing attention to oneself, and the moment you draw attention to yourself, you are taking it away from Jesus.

The methods by which the offerings are often received are designed to honor the flesh, and totally rob the poor soul from the reward of God. I have heard evangelists say that God told them that ten people were going to give a thousand dollars that night, then would rant and rave and threaten the people until the ten were standing to their feet. As each would stand, attention would be given to him or her, and applause would be encouraged. As the crowd applauded I felt sick in my heart, and I thought, "Enjoy it and take it in, poor soul, for this will be the only reward you will receive for that gift." As Jesus said, "You have your reward." I also felt anger toward the pastor or evangelist who would encourage people to give in such a way as to receive no reward from God. I also felt that he lied when he declared that God had told him how many people were going to give a thousand dollars. That is nothing more than a psychological ploy.

Distasteful Ploys

Equally distasteful are the other psychological ploys that are used to solicit funds to support the work of God. Many of the charismatic evangelists have developed mailing lists, and with the use of computer typewriters they send out their mass mailings to their gullible followers, many of whom are deceived into thinking that they are receiving a personal letter from dear Brother _____ (famous-name healing evangelist), for the computer has repeated their name many times in the body of the letter. The letters are filled with lies, as they often say, "The Lord laid you on my heart this morning to pray especially for you. Is something wrong? Please write me and tell me your need so I can help you."

In 2 Peter 2 we are told that one sign of a false prophet is that he will use feigned words to make merchandise of the people. These letters fit Peter's description perfectly. They so often appeal to the flesh. If you want answers to your prayers, or a special work of God, then plant your seed gift. These methods deny the grace of God, since you are supposedly buying God's favor. It has always puzzled me how these men who have learned all the secrets of faith and have such great power with God never seem to have enough faith to trust God to take care of their *own* needs, but warn that God's work is going to fail unless the people come to His aid immediately and save Him from bankruptcy.

What You Say Is What You Get?

The latest wind of pernicious, unscriptural doctrine to blow through the ranks of some charismatics is the "what-you-say-is-what-you-get" teaching, otherwise known as the prosperity doctrine. Among the claims that are commonly made is that God never wills that you should be sick and that all sickness is the result of ignorance or lack of faith. Such teachings sound more like Mary Baker Eddy than the Apostle Paul!

These people speak much of making positive confessions, and warn against any negative confession. They teach that the spoken word becomes a spirit force for good or evil according to the confession. Thus you are never to confess, "I don't feel well," for that is a negative confession and is bound to cause you to feel bad. You are thus encouraged to lie about your true condition or feelings. As you hear this teaching you would swear that the sermons came from *Science and Health with Key to the Scriptures* rather than the Bible.

I have heard such people seek to explain away Paul's thorn in the flesh by saying, "Where else do we find thorns in the Bible?" "Jesus," they said, "spoke of the thorns choking out the Word so that the seed could not produce." Now what were these thorns? The cares of this life, the deceitfulness of riches, and the lust for other things. Therefore Paul's thorn in the flesh was the cares of life that he took upon himself.

Had these people bothered to do the slightest amount of research, they would have discovered that there are two entirely different Greek words translated "thorns" in these passages. The word that Paul used about his thorn in the flesh was a Greek word that referred to a tent stake, not some nagging little irritation. Paul spoke to the Galatians about his infirmities; the English word has the same root as "infirmary," or what we call a hospital.

One of these charismatic leaders said to me, "Inasmuch as this was given to Paul lest he be exalted above measure, don't you think that if Paul could have just conquered his flesh, the thorn would not have been necessary?" I cannot imagine the spiritual pride insinuated by such a remark. In essence, he was declaring that he had conquered over his flesh more thoroughly than Paul. This surely was not apparent by the flashy clothes, car, and home that he possessed. Yet he said that all of this lavish living was just a sign of his faith, for if God could trust us with money, He wanted us all to prosper, and anyone with enough faith could live like the King's kid.

What does that say about Jesus, who had no place to lay His head, and had to send Peter fishing in order to get a coin to pay the taxes? I know of many people who have died while making their positive confessions of healing. Some of them could have been helped by competent medical care, but to go to a doctor would be a negative confession and an admission that something was wrong. In other cases I know of people who followed the lies of the positive-confession evangelists, and when their confessions failed to materialize, they turned their backs on God completely. I also know that some of the evangelists who are the chief exponents of this positive confession as the way to constant health and continuous prosperity have spent time in the hospital for nervous exhaustion.

The people who seem to have prospered the most from these teachings are the evangelists themselves. How will they answer to God for conning the poor little widow out of half her Social Security check, causing her to miss several meals for lack of funds so they can fly in their private jets to their luxury condominiums in Palm Springs and dine in the plushest restaurants?

Paul writes to Timothy about the perverse teachings of men of corrupt minds who are destitute of the truth, for they suppose that godliness is a way to prosperity. Paul warned Timothy to stay away from them. This is a free but accurate translation of the Greek text in 1 Timothy 6:5. Paul then told Timothy that godliness with contentment was great riches.

12

Receiving the Power

There are often obstacles to receiving this special anointing or power of the Holy Spirit in your life which must be overcome! First is a general sense of unworthiness. Satan, fulfilling his role as the accuser of the brethren, will try to exaggerate our failures and mistakes, and he intimates that we are not worthy to receive anything from God. In one sense this is true; however, God does not give us His gifts as a reward for good behavior, but to enable us to live a life pleasing to Him. The power of the Holy Spirit is the very power that I need to help me live a victorious life in Christ. Also, inasmuch as it is a gift from God, He gives it on the basis of His grace and not my merit.

Another obstacle is unscriptural anticipations that we may have developed from preconceived ideas which are often planted by the testimony of someone else's experience. For years I thought that, when I received the empowering of the Spirit, I would lapse into an unconscious state or some kind of trance. I had heard the testimonies of those who were filled with the Spirit, and they often declared, "...and when I came to, I was surprised to discover I had been there for four hours." Thus, while tarrying for the Holy Spirit, I often waited in vain to lapse into some unconscious state. Others would testify of various sensations, such as "ten thousand volts of electricity passing through my body" or "a warm sensation came over me." Still others described the continuous waves of glory sweeping over them or the tingling sensation down their spine. Some told of uncontrollable weeping, while others spoke of violent shaking.

All of these may be valid reactions to the work or power of the Spirit upon a person's life, but the wide variety only shows that God is not bound to any pattern in bestowing the gift of the Holy Spirit upon our lives. We should not anticipate any special kind of sensation as proof that God has filled us with His Spirit apart from that full flooding of love, for the fruit of the Spirit is love.

Quite often, if I am anticipating some special kind of reaction or sensation, I am disappointed when I do not receive it, and I feel that God has not bestowed His gift upon me. I am prone to doubt my own experience, or lack of it, and take it as God's refusal to bless me.

Ask and Receive

If we are to receive the gift of the Holy Spirit, we must ask. In Luke 11:13 Jesus said, "How much more will your heavenly Father give the Holy Spirit to those who ask Him?" Asking is a very important part of receiving. In James 4:2 we are told that we have not because we ask not. Many people are lacking the power of God's Spirit in their lives today simply because they have never asked. In John 15:16 Jesus said to His disciples, "You did not choose me, but I chose you and ordained you, that you should go and bring forth fruit, and that your fruit should remain; that whatever you shall ask the Father in my name, He may give it to you." Notice that Jesus said, "He *may* give," not "He *shall* give." It is something that God has purposed to do already, and the asking just opens the door for Him to do what He is longing to do for you.

In John 16:24 Jesus said, "Ask and you shall receive, that your joy may be full." The Spirit-filled life is full of joy. Joy is the first word Paul uses to define the love which is the fruit of the Spirit (Galatians 5:22). In 1 John 5:14,15 we are told that, if we ask anything according to God's will, He hears us, and if He hears us, then we have the petitions that we desired of Him. Is it God's will that we be filled with the Spirit? We know it is, for God commanded it in Ephesians 5:18: "Be ye being filled with the Spirit." When I ask that God fill me with the Spirit, I have that confidence of knowing that I am asking according to His will.

Anything I ask of God I must ask in faith, believing that God will do it. So my next step must be the step of faith; I must believe that God has done it. Faith is the substance of things hoped for, the evidence of things not seen. Faith is all the evidence you need; believe that you receive it, and you shall have it. We need not look for any immediate sign such as tongues, hot flashes, or waves of glory. They may occur, but not necessarily, and I should not look for some feeling as proof that God has granted my prayer. Our faith must always rest in the sure Word of God, and never in a feeling. Our feelings often change, but never God's Word.

Paul asked the Galatian believers, "Received ye the Spirit by the works of the law or by the hearing of faith?" The same is true in our lives. The filling of the Spirit is not some reward that God gives me for meritorious service, but just the pure gift of His grace. In Romans 4:20 we read that, because

Abraham was strong in faith, he gave glory to God. Ask God now to fill you with His Holy Spirit, and begin to exercise your faith by praising God now for that new dynamic of love He is pouring into your life.

13

A More Excellent Way

We read in Galatians 5 about the spiritual battle that is going on in every Christian. This battle does not take place in the non-Christian; he does not know anything about it, because the spirit of the non-Christian is dormant.

But once your spirit has come alive, once you have been born again, there is an internal conflict. In Galatians 5:17 Paul said, "For the flesh lusts against the spirit and the spirit against the flesh, and these are contrary to each other, so that you cannot do the things that you would." The battle that is going on is the spirit versus the flesh; the flesh is keeping you from doing those things that you want to do for the Lord. "Now the works of the flesh are manifest, which are these: adultery, fornication, uncleanness, lasciviousness, idolatry, witchcraft, hatred, variance, emulations, wrath, strife, seditions, heresies, envyings, murders, drunkenness, revelings, and the like: of which I tell you before, as I have also told you in times past, that those who do such things shall not inherit the kingdom of God" (verses 19-21).

In marked contrast to the works of the flesh are the results of the Spirit: "The fruit of the Spirit is love [agape]" (verse 22). The method of God is fruit in contrast to works. Any time you get in the realm of *works,* you are getting in the realm of the flesh.

But *fruit*, indicating to us the method of God, is the natural consequence of a relationship. You do not see an apricot tree struggling and straining to produce apricots, nor do you see the apricots struggling and straining to get ripe; it is just a natural process.

How to Bear Fruit

God's method for you is just the natural process of God working in your life—it is not something that you can do, that you strain and struggle to try to develop. The minute you get into that straining and struggling, you are in the realm of works again. God's method is fruit, and the fruit is the natural consequence of the relationship of abiding in Christ.

Jesus said, "I am the vine and you are the branches. Every branch in me that brings forth fruit, the Father purges it [or cleanses it, washes it] that it might bring forth more fruit. Now you are cleansed through the word that I have spoken to you; abide in me and let my words abide in you." As you abide in Christ, you are going to bear fruit. Jesus said, "You cannot bear fruit unless you abide in the vine." The branch cannot produce fruit by itself. You have got to abide in the vine if you are going to bear fruit. Jesus also said, "Apart from me you can do nothing." But as you abide in Christ, the natural result is that His love will begin to flow forth from your life. The method of God is fruit—the very easy, very natural consequence of just abiding in Jesus.

The word "Spirit" in "the fruit of the Spirit" indicates to us the dynamic of God—the work of the Holy Spirit within the life of the believer. It is no accident that 1 Corinthians chapter 13 is sandwiched between Paul's discussion of the gifts of the Spirit in chapters 12 and 14. In chapter 12 he lists many of the gifts of the Spirit; in chapter 14 he describes how some of these gifts operate, and the purposes of some of these gifts. But at the end of chapter 12 he says, "I will show you a more excellent way"—something even more excellent than the possession of these marvelous gifts.

The Excellent Way

Often we say, "Oh God, I want the gift of miracles" or "I want the gift of faith" or "I want the gift of healing" or "I want the gift of diiscernment of spirits" or "I want the gift of the word of knowledge." We would like to have these supernatural gifts operating in our lives. But Paul said, "I'll show you a more excellent way." Even more than having the supernatural gifts operating in my life, it is preferable to have God's love flowing from my life, and if that love is not flowing, these supernatural gifts become meaningless.

"The fruit of the Spirit" indicates to us the dynamic of God. Jesus said, "You shall receive power [dunamis] after the Holy Spirit is come upon you." The Holy Spirit is God's dynamic within our lives. He is that power within us who gives us the ability to be what we could not be apart from Him, and to have what we cannot have apart from Him, and to do what we could not do apart from Him. You cannot have the agape without the Holy Spirit, and you cannot express the agape without the Holy Spirit. The fruit of God's Spirit within your life is that this love will come forth. The natural outflow of the Spirit of God within you will be this love, for the Spirit of God is the dynamic force of God within you that produces this agape from your life. The method of God is fruit; the dynamic of God is the Spirit.

The Real Fruit of the Spirit

You have probably heard that there are nine fruits of the Spirit. I have heard messages on the nine gifts of the Spirit and the nine fruits of the Spirit. But I want you to look closely at Galatians 5:22: "The fruit of the Spirit *is agape*." As I understand English grammar and as I understand Greek grammar, if there were nine fruits Paul would have said, "But the *fruits* of the Spirit *are* love, joy, peace, etc."

But that is not what he said. It is in the singular: "The fruit of the Spirit *is* love." Then what are these other things in the verse? What about the joy, the peace, the long suffering, the gentleness, the goodness, the faith, the meekness, and the temperance? These are all defining the agape. Our English usage of the word "love" is so weak that it can mean almost anything. So Paul defines this agape by using these other words.

Joy is love's consciousness. Have you ever seen a person really in love? The chief characteristic of that person is the joy he or she has. Oh what joy there is in true love! You can face some of the toughest situations and still have true joy. You can be doing some of the most miserable tasks, but if there is true love, there is glorious joy. Talking with a young girl a while back I asked, "Well, how are you doing?" She replied, "Oh, I'm doing great! I just got married and I don't have to work anymore." She meant that she did not have to work from 8 to 5 behind a desk. She was probably doing more work than she had ever done, but now there was such love that she did not even count it as work. Love makes every task a pleasure. When you truly love, you do not get uptight over things you do for those you love. You enjoy doing them. Joy is love's consciousness.

The second characteristic of the Spirit's agape is *peace*. There can be no true peace apart from agape love. Someone said, "There is now peace in the Middle East." Don't you believe it! There is no peace at all. There is so much hatred; there is so much bitterness. There isn't any real peace there. At a moment's notice the whole thing could blow into a full-scale war. The only true basis for peace is love. You can have a cessation of hostilities; you can have truces; you can have agreements; but the only true basis for peace is real love. When I love you so much that I would not want to do anything that would harm you in any way, then we have peace between us.

Longsuffering. Paul used this word in his definition of agape in 1 Corinthians 13: "Love is long-suffering and kind." If you truly love someone, you do not keep track of how many times you have been offended. You are longsuffering. You take and take and take, and then you are kind.

Another characteristic of agape is its *gentleness:* Oh how gentle is love! What a beautiful quality, what an admirable quality, is the gentleness of true love!

Then *goodness.* I believe that love is the only real motive for goodness. A lot of people are good only because they fear the consequences of being bad. But that is not true goodness. "I'd like to murder you but I'd get jailed." "I'd like to rob that bank but I might get caught." A lot of people are restrained from evil only for the fear of the consequences. That is not goodness. The only true motivation for goodness is love. Because of love, I would not want to hurt and I would not want to offend. I would do nothing to cause a person to stumble, because I love that person. That's the true motivation for goodness.

Another characteristic of agape is *faith.* This is not the same faith that we find as a gift of the Spirit in 1 Corinthians 12, but it is a faith or trust in *people.*

It is just a "trustingness." If you say, "I don't trust anybody," you are just saying, "I don't love anybody." If you truly love a person, you will trust him, because trusting is a part of the quality of agape love.

And then there is *meekness*. True love does not seek its own way, does not vaunt itself, and is not puffed up. One of the chief characteristics of Jesus Christ is His beautiful meekness. He could have been on a big power trip when He was here. After all, look who He was. Often Jesus referred to Himself with the title "the Son of Man." He had many glorious titles that He could have taken: the Son of Righteousness, the Son of Glory, the Bright and Morning Star, the Fairest of Ten Thousand, the Lily of the Valley, the Wonderful Counselor, the Mighty God, the Everlasting Father, the Prince of Peace. All of these are proper titles that Jesus could have taken. He could have said "The Bright and Morning Star saith unto thee" or "The Anointed of God declares...." But instead He often referred to Himself as the Son of Man: "The Son of Man has come to seek and to save that which was lost."

Many people today honor one another with their fancy titles. How people love titles! But Jesus disdained titles; He put down those who loved to stand in the marketplace being called "Rabbi, Rabbi!" Someone once said that titles are only distinctions by which we tell one worm from another. What am I? *Nothing* apart from God. Love's characteristic is that of meekness.

Finally, *temperance*. The best way I can think of to define temperance is to give the opposite: *intemperance*. Unfortunately we know all too well what that is, and it is the opposite of temperance. Temperance is moderation, not going overboard. It is that beautiful evenness of love.

The Fruit in Your Life

This agape love is what the Holy Spirit is seeking to bring into your life; agape is the true fruit of the Spirit. This will be the final result of God's Spirit dwelling in you. As God's Spirit works within you, and as you yield yourself to the Spirit, the fruit of the Spirit is agape love. The purpose of the work of the Holy Spirit within your life as a believer is to do for you what you cannot do for yourself—bring to you that agape love of God for the family of God.

This will be a sign by which the world will know that you are Christ's disciple, and a sign by which you will know that you have passed from death to life. It is a sign because you will see God's love working in your life.

We need to be filled with the Spirit. We need to yield to the Spirit so that His fruit might come forth abundantly from our lives. Then we will have His agape love ruling us, flowing forth from our lives like a torrent of living water.

14

A Final Word

One of the sad results of *charismania* is its repelling influence on so many hungry, earnest saints of God who are needing and searching for a deeper experience of God's power in their lives.

We read in 2 Kings 4 that Elisha, during a famine, sought to feed the sons of the prophets by setting before them a great seething pot into which they had placed the herbs that they had gathered. One of the young prophets had shredded wild gourds into the pottage so that when they sought to satisfy their hunger by eating they cried out, "There is death in the pot!"

This is what often happens when a person, hungry for the fullness of God, tastes of the noxious wildfire of the *charismaniacs*. They unfortunately conclude that there is no genuine work of God's Spirit in the church today, and they continue to struggle with their Christian walk without the help of the full dynamic of the Holy Spirit.

God did not intend the children of Israel to die in the wilderness, but to come into the overflowing abundance of the Promised Land. God does not intend that your walk with Him be a dry, barren wilderness experience, but He desires that you come to know the full richness of that life promised to us through the Holy Spirit.

Do not allow the unscriptural excesses of those practicing *charismania* to discourage you from seeking all that God wants you to experience of the love, joy, and power of living in the fullness of the Spirit. We have not yet experienced the full, rich spectrum of the genuine work of the Spirit in our lives; thus we need to always remain open to God for whatever He may desire to bestow upon us. There is so much in the Scriptures which we have not yet experienced that we certainly have no need to go beyond the Scriptures.

Paul expressed his joy that the Corinthian church did not lack or come short of any spiritual gift as they awaited the coming of Jesus. So my prayer is that we also may experience all of the fullness of the Holy Spirit and the gifts that He desires to bestow upon us as we wait for our Lord's return.